People,

Poetry,

Prose

2023 Anthology
By Tamarack Writers' Group
Lakeview, Michigan USA 48850

ISBN 13: 978-1-62329-116-7
ISBN 10: 1-62329-116-X

© 2024 this edition Mercer Publications & Ministries, Inc., Publisher
Stanwood, Michigan U.S.A.

Individual works copyrighted by their authors.

Copying is prohibited, except for brief excerpts for review, without the permission of the individual authors and Tamarack Writers' Group.

Edited by Dorothy May Mercer
and Kathryn Nerychel

© 2024 Tamarack Writers' Group, Lakeview, Michigan

Acknowledgements:

Tamarack Writers' Group
Tamarack District Library, Lakeview, Michigan

Numerous interior photos and artwork by Unknown Authors are licensed under CC, BY,CC BY-ND, and under CC BY-SA-NC

Featuring
Tamarack Writers' Group
Lakeview, Michigan:

Tom Colburn
Raeanna Davidson
Linda Hawley
Chuck Houghton
Priscilla Jeffers
Gerald "Jake" Kinsey
Dorothy May Mercer
Kathy Nerychel
Gail Shenemen
Marian Stockwell
Charleen Stroup
E.L. "Luke" Ward
Janice Wilson

In Memorium

Janice Wilson
Feb. 28, 1957 -- April 13,2024

Table Of Contents

Nature 1

Moon Shining 2
Linda Hawley 2
Monday Morning Silence 4
Dorothy May Mercer 4
Snowstorm 6
Dorothy May Mercer 6
Winter Aerobics 6
Kathy Nerychel 6
My Gentile Allouette 8
Janice Wilson 8
Birds 9
Janice Wilson 9
A Snowball's Chance 10
Janice Wilson 10
Memories of Janice Wilson 12
Priscilla Jeffers 12
The First Day of Spring 15
Charleen Stroup 16
Sunshine 15
Raeanna Davidson 15
Fun 18
Raeanna Davidson 18
Mystery 20
Linda Hawley 20
Setting Sun 21
Gail Shenemen 21

Experiences 25

Relax?!? 27
Marian Stockwell 27
Going to the Mill 32
Dorothy May Mercer 32
Tuesday at the Bank 36
C.J.'s in Howard City 39
Linda Hawley 39
Rare Blessings 40
Gail Sheneman 40
Quiet 45
Linda Hawley 45
Cow Pasture 46
Linda Hawley 46
Learning to Drive in Lakeview 48
Kathy Nerychel 48

Four Strong Women 51
Dorothy May Mercer 51
Country Girl /City Girl 52
Marian Stockwell 52
Morning Person 57
Kathy Nerychel 57
The Garage Across from Imperial 58
Linda Hawley 58
Jigsaw Puzzles for Brain Improvement 60
Dorothy May Mercer 60
"New Math" 64
Linda Hawley 64
Picking Zucchini 66
Kathy Nerychel 66
The Give and Take of Phases 67
Dorothy May Mercer 67
Eighty-three 68
Gail Shenemen 68
I Never Would Have Believed This
Gail Shenemen 70
Stay in Quarantine 74
Raeanna Davidson 74
Anticipating a Storm 75
Linda Hawley 75
Daddy Back 76
Kathy Nerychel 76
I Cry Out 79
Raeanna Davidson 79
Two Religious Experiences on St. Thomas 80
Kathy Nerychel 80
Empty Nest – Full Heart 84
Gail Shenemen 84

Advice 85

Spice of Life 87
Marian Stockwell 87
New Hope 91
Linda Hawley 91
The Gift for Me 92
Charleen Stroup 92
Math or Arithmetic? 94
Gail Sheneman' 94
I Promise You 95
Gail Sheneman 95

v

Pets 97

Esmeralda 98
Linda Hawley 98
The New Kitty 99
Gail Shenemen 99
Herding Cats 100
Kathy Nerychel 100
Kitty 102
Linda Hawley 102
Cat # 2 103
Gail Shenemen 103
Live Like You're Not 104
Gail Sheneman 104
Gifts 106
Linda Hawley 106

Fiction 107

Vittorio: Messages in my head 108
Tom Colburn 108
Sunday Dinner with Sharon 117
Dorothy May Mercer 117

Observations 123

I Watch the News 124
Dorothy May Mercer 124
Weeds 125
Linda Hawley 125
November 126
Gail Sheneman 126
Old Age 127
Raeanna Davidson 127
Words 128
Charleen Stroup 128
Heavenly Love 129
Raeanna Davidson 129

Holidays 131

Easter Bunnies 132
Gail Sheneman 132
Daylight Saving Time 133
Gail Sheneman 133
A Letter to My Pen pal in Nigeria, 134
Dorothy May Mercer 134
Halloween Night 136
Linda Hawley 136

Funny Thanksgiving Story in 260 Words 137
Dorothy May Mercer 137
Thanksgiving Blessing 138
Raeanna Davidson 138
Veterans's Day Memories 139
Dorothy May Mercer 139
Serving Our Country 140
Raeanna Davidson 140
Jake's Christmas Editorial 141
Gerald Kinsey 141
Snowed Under ❄ 145
Raeanna Davidson 145
2024 Resolution 146
Gail Shenemen 146

People 147

The Auctioneer 148
Dorothy May Mercer 148
Earliest Memories of My Only Living Grandma 154
Dorothy May Mercer 154
Oh, My Ron! 156
Linda Hawley 156
Bob Hawley 157
Linda Hawley 157
Mr. Negativity 158
Gail Shenemen 158
Butch and Marlene 159
Linda Hawley 159
Shelley and Pastor Ron 160
Linda Hawley 160
Kathy 161
Gail Shenemen 161
Molly 162
Gail Shenemen 162
Elegy for Bethy 164
Gail Shenemen 164

Imagine 165

The Two Murders 166
E.L. Ward 166
Four Limericks 182
Dorothy May Mercer 182
Fly 183
Gail Sheneman 183

Nature

Moon Shining

Linda Hawley

Round silvery moon shining
Over library Monday night
Witness to a bright sight
Always rising and climbing

Moon peaking through branches
Seeking sometimes to hide
But so full of pride
What are the chances?

Soon will be out of sight
Moment by moment keep watching
This moon will be launching
Moving swiftly through the night

Linda

Linda Hawley is inspired by her mother who published two books. Linda enjoys writing about her childhood in Lakeview. She crochets, embroiders, and plays the piano.

Monday Morning Silence

Dorothy May Mercer

This morning Dave is gone
Driving o'er to Remes
Leaving a lonely vacuum
Of resonating silence

Close on the nearby pane
A tapping on the window
Sleet and freezing rain!
An avalanche of wet snow

Too quiet while I wait
An anxious test of faith
He's here! Unharmed, though late
Give thanks to God, he's safe

"It was a slippery drive,"
He said. "Impossible to see
I'm thankful I'm alive
And home at last with Thee."

Dorothy

Dorothy May Mercer is a writer and retired music teacher. She likes to help other authors with their books, and so she enjoys Tamarack Writer's Group. She was instrumental with the publication of this anthology. Her hobbies include gardening, boating, and playing the piano.

She is the author of numerous books including novels, travelogues, and "How To" books. Her most recent publications include the Kindle Vella "Pastor B and the Haunted Church" She lives in Michigan with her husband Dave. They named their cat "Kitty" on the theory that if he ever got lost, someone might call him saying, "Here Kitty, here Kitty."

Snowstorm

Dorothy May Mercer

Their sidewalk, deck and drive were banked in flakes.
Another zillion landed on the lakes.
Due to shoveling her back now akes.

(A Diminishing Verse Poem, meaning you remove the first letter of the last word in line one for each subsequent line. Example lines 1-3 end in flakes, lakes, and akes.)

Winter Aerobics

Kathy Nerychel

The lilac bush is touching its toes.
Utility lines are lifting icicle weights.
Branches are carrying an icy blanket.
Frozen branches need to flex or break.
Mother Nature is exercising her ice storm power.

Kathy

Kathy Nerychel, a retired Title I teacher from Lakeview Schools, enjoys writing. She took part in the National Writing Project at Ferris State University, dreamed of joining a writer's group, and started Tamarack Writer's Group. She loves to spend time with grandchildren, travel and garden.

My Gentile Allouette

Janice Wilson

I was a small girl in Quebec
Who loved to sing a song of a bird's neck
I sang it so much
As teacher told me this such
But I hardly understood a speck.

My teacher taught me this song.
The length of this song was quite long.
It describes a bird's beauty,
A North American cutie,
An old Canadian folksong.

Watching the birds at my window
As they perform a beautiful calypso.
Each gentile allouette
A magnificent epithet
Especially after a first snow.

Birds

Janice Wilson

I chant of their feathers
While they perch among heathers.
To see swift wings flap
And splitting seeds as they tap
Bringing joy to my friends of fair weathers.

Singing of a beautiful songbird
I simply learned every French word,
As the word for beak.
A fun language to speak,
My parents this song constantly heard.

Many years I have trekked
Seeing allouette[1] as the birds peck.
Paws, back and tails
Cute males and females
As I grow old is this girl from Quebec.

---

[1] Allouette is a French word meaning lark. Also, it is the name of an old folk tune.

A Snowball's Chance

Janice Wilson

My drives to the big city are usually dull.
My thoughts become scattered as I begin to mull.
Taking in my surroundings between walls of snow
I aspired to negate boredom, while preventing woe.

The analogy of an expanding snowball came to mind.
My continual revolving thoughts I would try to unwind.
Imagine a snowball effect, put it in reverse.
Am I able to back track to my initial converse?

Attempts to discover prior abstractions
Caused many unexpected reactions.
My efforts to find the route to my thoughts
Were in vain, my recollections were knots.

The drive to the big city wasn't doldrum that day.
And I realized its easier to let my thoughts stray.
My attempts to reverse my thoughts didn't conspire

Janice Wilson showed great promise as a poet and writer. She was enthused about these three poems and rightly so. Clearly, she loved to sing and enjoyed the bird songs.

We mourn her sudden passing in April, 2023.

Janice Wilson lived in Edmore and enjoyed writing poetry. She was new to Tamarack Writers and so, unfortunately, these three introspective poems are all we have of her work.

Memories of Janice Wilson
Friend, Mom, Grandmother, Sister, and Pet-Owner
Priscilla Jeffers

Friend- Janice was a good friend. She took strides helping others in any way she could. Reaching out to people who were in need that there was a food truck coming, or where to find the pantry. Giving rides to some who needed to go to the Walk-In clinic. Her love language was giving and she often gave thoughtful gifts to brighten one's day. When she received a gift she was delighted and her eyes would sparkle.

Mom- Janis cared very much for her two children. Her son Chris his wife Danielle and her own daughter, Danielle. She was very proud of their accomplishments and often talked of their abilities as Army Recruiter, School teacher, Hospital Staff, and parents. She loved to hear Chris sing and made endeavors to go and hear him wherever he was singing.

Grandmother- Janice always put her grandchildren first, she rarely missed a game or special event. She would travel to Arizona once a year to visit her daughter and grandchildren; and leaving them at the end of the visit was difficult. Birthdays were especially important to her, she put great effort into finding the gift that would suit them best. She made them homemade cards and included many fun facts about them. Facts such as on the day you were born this or that happened. When Josh and Noah were Baptized it was a big deal to her. Again a thoughtful card was made and they both received a custom engraved compass to guide them on their way. Her granddaughter, Abby, was precious as were they all. She kept toys and games at her house for them and made sure Abby had plenty of dolls to play with. She liked to take them fishing and loved going to the lake. Janice loved water and would often speak of her father's role in that. She remembered her parents fondly and often mentioned that she had had a wonderful childhood. She wished to give her grandchildren the type of love that her parents gave to her.

Sister- Sunday evenings were for her siblings who would do a four-way call to discuss their current happenings. She was also very proud of them. They still live in Canada so the call was a wonderful way for them to keep in touch.

Pet owner- Janice's pets were very important to her. When she came back from Arizona, her cat had died and she felt bad for not being there for her. A stray dog came into her yard one day. She called to see who the owners were and found that they no longer wanted him. She thought he'd be a good pet for the kids to play with when they came by. So, Janice named him Leo and took him in as her dog. She had him for just a few years. She cared for his health issues and even made him nutritional homemade dog food. Leo started to have back and hip problems and soon it was evident that his quality of life had diminished to the point that she had him put-down. She did not let her disabilities keep her from getting on the floor and holding him through the process. She cuddled him and told him it was going to be ok and that she loved him very much. She took great care in picking out the perfect urn to "bring him back home" with her.

Janice knew that this world was not her home. She knew that her real home was in heaven in the arms of her savior, Jesus Christ. Where family and friends that have gone on before her were waiting and her faithful pets came running. A grand reunion must have been had by all.

Priscilla

Priscilla Jeffers is a local author who has studied the meaning of flowers. She has written a historical novel, *When the Redbud Blooms,* and enjoys writing poetry.

Sunshine

Raeanna Davidson

Sunshine on a cloudy day
Foggy day on a rainy day
But sunshine takes all the rain away.

The moon is so bright,
That the stars of night come
From above the heavens.

In the clouds by night and day
The stars shine bright enough,
That they can light up the entire world
Under the stars or under the heavens.

The First Day of Spring

Charleen Stroup

I thought this was supposed to be
The first of spring in Michigan.
Last night I see it snowed again;
The ground is white, the roads icy.

If you're from here, you may agree
This just might be an Irish joke,
Or maybe from an English bloke.
Well that fell flat - with a big thud.
But then, again, better than flood!
So, hand me now my winter coat.

Charleen

Charleen "Charlie" Stroup is new to writing and is publishing her first book. As a retired nurse and mental health counselor, she now has more time to spend on her hobbies of gardening, craft, painting, music, and volunteering. After growing up in Michigan and spending 33 years in Florida, she recently returned to Big Rapids to be near her family.

Fun

Raeanna Davidson

In the spring the sun is fun.
The sportsman's passion is in the sun.
The jazzman plays in the sun.
A craftsman makes things in the sun.
Children run in the sun.

Raeanna

Raeanna

Raeanna Davidson loves hanging out with her family. She loves soccer and helping all the people that need her help. She also loves riding her golf cart all over town. You will always see her smiling. She loves to write books for little children all around the world.

Mystery

Linda Hawley

One hundred geese
Two hundred geese
Were resting at pickle docks.
Now Byrne docks
Is there a limit to their number?
Is this also where they slumber?
Been happening year after year.
How do they happen to appear?
Who tells who?
There is no clue.

Setting Sun

Gail Shenemen

I lie, afraid to close my eyes,
lest I miss the last few shreds of daylight.
I see the trees, majestic silhouettes,
against the radiant glow of the setting sun.

In the east the sky grows gray
and in the west
sinks the last of day.

Gail

Gail Shenemen has written a children's book, **The Princess and the Little Elephant,** and has books of poetry and memoirs in the works. She also enjoys art, collecting, and choir and country singing. She is a tenor and has sung in six different choirs, including the Michigan-Ohio Concert Choir in Detroit.

Gail and her second husband, Carl, love to dance when they can. She raised six children, one of whom passed away at age 47, has 15 grandchildren and makes her home in Montcalm County. Buddy, Katie, and Sallie, her three cats, are her babies now.

Before her retirement, Gail achieved degrees from three different educational institutions, and held careers in chiropractic, architecture, real estate, and teaching.

She intends to keep right on going - until she can't.

Drawing by Kim Bunch, illustrator

Experiences

Relax?!?

Marian Stockwell

Relax you say? Does it count if I relax after playing pickleball, swimming, or going to the gym? I sure wish I could; relax that is. While lounging one beautiful day at the poolside with my friend Renu, I was eye-balling the pool. I need to exercise, I told myself, half-listening to her talk about what she had done the previous day. "You're thinking about getting back into the pool again, aren't you? You just got done swimming laps."

Caught red-handed, I had to fess up, "Yes, I guess I have a lot of energy to burn."

"You need to relax, truly relax, clear your mind."

I might add that my friend Renu is from India, and I'll bet meditation and relaxation might come easier for her! "Maybe I should join a yoga class?!"

"You go to the gym, the Needlecraft shop, the Photo club, you swim laps, have started line dancing, and now you want yoga classes to fix you."

"Yeah" and then I thought, It only makes sense, that is the class that is supposed to teach you to relax, right?

"You need to look within, to let your mind and body rest, you need rest, relaxation."

"Well teach me," I answered logically. To me, relaxing comes after you have run yourself ragged and then it is crash and burn time. Mind you, I do not like to nap and only indulge when I am sick, too many fun things I might miss. But somehow, I don't think that is what she meant, wiped out to the point of barely functioning.

What a waste of time my subconscious whispers in my ear. *Just sitting, not thinking, not planning, not sleeping, that's crazy. Me, I'm going to do yogurt, not yoga!*

Illustration by Kim Bunch)

Back into the conversation, I hear her say, "The class I'm going to is chair yoga. Most is done in a chair. You wouldn't believe how much you stretch out your muscles."

By this time, I am laughing inside. How hard can it be? What kind of workout is that, in a chair!? Not for me! I'm thinking. How do you burn off those calories and get those feel-good endorphins from a chair for gosh sakes?

"You can come and try it once for free and then decide if you want to join." Well, maybe that would do me some good, better than an advanced yoga class. I am so tight in my back and just about all of my muscles. Trying to do those pretzel-poses they would end up going BIIIINGG, just like a rubber band snapping. Now to think of it, I have difficulty getting up from

28

the floor, they would be done with the class, and I would just be pulling myself up after crawling to the nearest chair. Back to the chair again, hmm. "You know, that might be a good idea after all, when is that class?"

"My sister Myra will call and leave a message. Call me when you aren't too busy running here and there." She is right I realize, I am usually gone, but Myra, just leave me a message and I will get back to you. It was brought to my attention that not everyone has the same definition of "relax", so I looked up the definition and here it is:

. Relax- to make or become less tense or anxious, less rigid.

So, there are many different ways to relax, everyone could potentially have their own activity or lack of which relaxes them. To some the perfect form of relaxation would be to sit in a comfortable chair at the beach, listening to waves or watching the sunset. To others and me, it might be good for a short time, maybe five minutes, and then we would be up walking the beach looking for seashells! It is hard for me to sit still unless I am reading a very good book.

There is also another factor to consider, besides individuality. What is relaxing to us can change, for example as we age. That is what is exciting about life. It doesn't have to be boring. When I returned to Florida (we are snowbirds) Renu and I rode our three-wheeler bikes up to the atrium (fancy word for clubhouse) and met at Cici's Café for tea and talked. This is why friends are so important, they want to help you and can be quite honest about what they observe. Renu could see how wound up I was. As we talked, her question came right to the point, "Can you change or fix what is happening? You already programmed your mind for the worse, negative thoughts, and are distressed. This is unhealthy for anyone. You have to train your mind to be positive, and to control your emotions through meditation, especially when you find yourself ready to "run". Give yourself five minutes, (I would have to start with a minute and a half, I am usually not able to wait even five minutes when I have something prodding me) only five minutes of mental rest to determine if your body and mind need to relax. Maybe read a book, drink a cup of coffee, work on a puzzle, whatever is relaxing to you." Relaxation will help with both your mental and physical well-being. Relaxation for me comes in the form of snorkeling in my living aquarium, the lake. While hanging in the water, the fish are not afraid and swim right past my view through a swim mask, as if in a parade! Ok, I'll try it, relaxation. I will try to participate in a few less activities. Excuse me for a minute while I go get my mug of coffee. Maybe I'll enjoy staying home so that I can "catch up" on all my neglected laundry, sweeping, organizing, and grocery shopping! Now I just realized why I don't like to relax, there's too much work to do while relaxing.

and it's not nearly as fun!

Marian

Marian Stockwell is a cancer survivor. She retired from teaching and working at a Hispanic Service Center. She was diagnosed with pancreatic cancer at the age of sixty-one. She went through surgery, chemotherapy, and radiation treatments, and is now enjoying life, snow birding with her husband Roger, between Michigan for the summers and Florida in the winters. She has written two books, available on Amazon, *Fighting the Odds Pancreatic Cancer and Me*, and her newest, *Still Here Pancreatic Cancer and Me*. Her latest book was illustrated by Kim Bunch. She also writes agricultural articles for the *Lakeview Area News*.

Going to the Mill

Dorothy May Mercer

While growing up on a farm in the 1930's, one of the simple pleasures was a trip to the mill. Dad would go to our granary, fill some gunny sacks with grain, and hitch the horses up to the wagon. On a lucky day, Daddy would take me along with him in the wagon.

Sometimes, Daddy allowed me to "help" fill the gunnysacks. Admittedly, my fun-filled antics were more of a hindrance than a help. While Dad shoveled the grain with a large, well-worn, dented, scoop-shovel, I entertained myself tromping in grain up to my knees, rolling, and sliding down an imaginary hill of grain, all the while kicking up a fragrant cloud of dust. Daddy was a tower of patience and never uttered a cussword beyond, "Goodness, Dorothy!"

Looking back, I imagine that experience helped to desensitize my sensory organs from any future allergies or asthma.

During the depths of the Great Depression, a farmer with a wife and four kids had almost no cash. Even though prices were fortunately a tiny fraction of what they are today, he needed to feed his family and animals from the produce of the farm.

My Dad grew food to feed our animals. The fields produced hay for the horses and four kinds of grain—wheat, oats, rye, and corn—to feed our chickens and cows, and sometimes the sheep and pigs.

32

There was a factory in every small farming community called a "mill." Usually, the mill was located on a dammed-up river where a large millwheel, turned by the force of the water, powered the equipment. Later when rural electrification arrived, millwheels became obsolete, but the mill's building stayed by the river.

The farmer took his grain to the mill to have it ground into feed for the farm animals. The mill would grind it into any formula that the farmer needed whether it was for chickens, or cows. Also, additives could be included according to the need. I'm guessing here, but I suppose the additives could be anything that the animal required from medicine to vitamins.

The grind could be any degree of coarseness, from very fine flour to granules. The resulting material was called "mash."

Finely ground flour would be for Mother, of course, to use in the kitchen to make pancakes, bread, biscuits, cakes, and cookies to feed the family.

After we arrived at the mill, the miller helped Dad unload the gunnysacks of grain and empty them into a large hopper. They allowed me to watch and observe so long as I "stayed out of trouble."

The miller was a jolly sort, dressed in dust-covered, bib overalls and blue denim shirt and hat. His eyelashes, eyebrows, and nose were covered in floury dust, as well. He promised me a sucker, if I behaved, and chuckled as he described the horror of what might happen to a bad boy or girl who accidentally fell into the hopper.

The dust that formed from the grain was peculiar, mostly white and with a pleasant odor like nowhere else. Sweet as it was, it could rapidly explode into a blazing inferno when set off by a spark. Because of that No Smoking signs were prominently posted and enforced. And the miller took precautions to keep his machinery clean and well-oiled.

The clanking sounds of the huge grinders as they engorged the grain and chewed it into bits were so loud, they drowned out conversation. I hovered back and covered my ears. Important instructions had to be yelled in the topmost voice or signed.

The miller tied clean bags to the ends of dual exhaust tubes and secured them there with special devices. At the right time, the finished mash would shoot into the exhaust tube which was the perfect size to hold a hundred pounds of mash. When full, the miller switched a damper on one end and opened it on the other, to allow a clean, new bag to fill. The miller closed the damper, unhooked the bag, sealed it tightly closed, and replaced the bag. Dad easily hefted one-hundred pounds onto his shoulder and placed it in the wagon, while the miller allowed the other bag to fill. This operation was repeated until all was finished.

At length, the machine was shut off and blessed silence restored, except for the persistent ringing in my ears. I followed Daddy and the miller into his office to "settle up." Dad seldom had the money, and so it fell to the proprietor to add the charges to the poor farmer's account.

Too shy to ask, I hoped that I would be rewarded with a sucker. Had I been "good" enough?

Mr. Miller-man enjoyed keeping me in suspense. Laughingly, he pretended to be indecisive and asked Dad what he thought. "What do you say, Leon? Does Dorothy deserve a sucker today?"

Daddy would reply, "Well, nobody's perfect, what do you think?"

"I'm in a generous mood today," Miller would say and hold out the Dum-dum suckers for my choice. My eyes would grow big at the magical choices: strawberry, lemon-lime, grape, raspberry, blueberry, and butterscotch, each one wrapped in a tiny cartoon paper, followed by a color-coded waxed paper. If possible, I would select my favorite, root-beer. But I knew it was rude to take too long or dig too deep.

"What do you say, Dorothy?" Daddy would ask, reminding me of my manners.

"Thank you, Mr. Miller," I would say as I unwrapped my delicious reward, popped it into my mouth, and read the cartoon.

Daddy boosted me onto the wagon, seated himself beside me, and grasped the reins.

"Giddyap," he would say, giving the horses a gentle slap on the butt with the reins, their signal to move forward toward home.

They knew the way.

Tuesday at the Bank

It was Tuesday morning about 10:30 and I was headed for the Mecosta County Senior Center for lunch and to play Euchre. Upon entering Remus, I remembered I needed money for the week, so I stopped at my bank. There was only a rather old black Chevrolet in the bank parking lot. I grabbed my cane and headed into the bank, smiling to myself, thinking about my latest joke that I pulled on my Republican friends: I say, "I'm going to stop playing Euchre."

"Why?' they ask. "You love Euchre."

I say, "Because I have to keep saying 'Trump.'"

As I entered the bank, something was wrong. The three lady tellers were piling money in front of themselves. No one said, "Good morning, Chuck."

At 84, I don't think very fast. Then I noticed the two males standing at each end of the row of teller booths had guns. "Put your pocketbook on the shelf, Gramps." was the order.

My stupid answer was, "I'm not here because it's "Donut Hole Day" at the bank. I don't have a dollar on me, and I don't have credit cards. I carry a picture of my dead daughter and that you'll never get."

He looked at me for a moment, "Sit down in that chair, Gramps and be quiet."

I did.

When I sat down in the chair, I slid the rubber end off my cane, and then I clicked my cell phone twice, which was very loud. The one man turned and looked at me. I had my open-ended cane pointed at him, which looked like a gun barrel. I asked, "did you hear the double click sound?"

"Yes," he said.

I said, "Please listen and don't either one of you move. My stepson is a mechanical engineer. He adapted my cane into a single-shot 10-gauge shotgun, which has one double shot buck- shot shell in it and we just heard me cock it."

"This handle is actually a pressure trigger. If you shoot me, my hand will relatch, and the cane will shoot."

"I shot this cane gun twice, and at this distance, I can pretty much disintegrate a 15-gallon pail. You're dead."

I soon learned they were brothers, and one didn't want to lose the other.

"Okay men, put your guns on the counter and lay down on the floor, face down. Someone, call the police."

I was standing by the desk with the donut holes on it. I ate one and looked at the clock: 10:50. I said to myself, "It's 10:50 on

37

Tuesday. Jake hasn't got the Lakeview Area News ready for print. I'm going to call him and give him a scoop on this spoiled bank robbery."

"Oh, what is that terrible irritating sound?"

Then I heard Sunshine yelling at me from the bathroom, "Turn off the alarm clock. It's Tuesday and we're going to the Senior Center for Euchre and lunch. Get ready! Now!"

Just one of my current real-life dreams.

C.J.'s in Howard City

Linda Hawley

I go there for breakfast
C. J.'s is my restaurant
With a welcoming storefront.

Service is the fastest.
A pancake is my favorite.
Go there to savor it.

Have it with sausage
Way above average
Experience is a delight.
Come by for a bite

Rare Blessings

Gail Sheneman

This year I have had more than my share of blessings. The first one happened in a Dollar General. I ran in to get a couple of items that I needed and when I went to pay for them, I couldn't find my debit card, or a credit card, or any money, and I was wasting everybody's time. A man spoke up and said, "I'll pay for it, just tell me how much it is."

I felt bad that I couldn't pay for it, but I thanked him and got out of the way. He said, "Don't worry about it; add it on to mine." It was fifteen dollars and something.

Not much, but it was to me; I appreciated it even though he was probably just getting me out of the way.

Another time I went to a doctor's appointment in Alma, which went well, and then stopped at Wal-Mart, found my purchases, then headed for check-out. Again, I could not find my debit card, no credit cards would work, my Sam's card, my Amazon Chase, or Capitol One. No check book, no cash. By this time everyone in line, including me, was getting frustrated. And I had left my phone at home, so I couldn't even call anyone. Especially the doctor's office where I had an upcoming appointment. I was in a quandary!

Then the lady behind me asked, "How much was the bill?"

The clerk and I both answered at once, "Sixty- something."

She said, "Put it on my bill; I'll pay it."

I said, "Really? You would do that? Then you'll have to give me your name and phone number so I can pay you back."

She answered, "Forget it; just do it for someone else; pay it forward."

And the clerk added it to her bill and she paid it. I hugged her tightly, and said, "You're an angel!" And as I did not get a receipt, I walked out with her.

I hurried back to Edmore, where I had already missed my appointment. When I had been in on Monday I had made an appointment for Wednesday, but the receptionist had not scheduled it, so I had not missed it after all. I explained why I was late, but she said, "It's not scheduled, so I can't charge you for missing it."

The next time I was late, and I tried to explain, he said I would have to wait until the next one, but I would also have to pay for the missed one, no explanations. The next time I was fifteen minutes early, but he had his mind made up. He wouldn't listen to anything I said. I said, "Most of the other doctors in this area call their patients with reminders of their appointments."

He said, "It's not going to happen! Takes too much time, somebody would have to do it, etc., not going to happen! We're all adults, and we can be responsible for ourselves. We can't continue like this or we're going to have to part ways!"

I paid the charge for being late plus the charge for that visit, and I haven't been back. He wouldn't take into consideration that we're all getting older and it's hard to remember at times. Having been the wife of the former owner and the designer of the building, you would think I should get some leeway. But that was a blessing in disguise and was of no consequence in the greater scheme of things. What the customer in Wal-Mart did for me far outweighed the lack of empathy from the doctor. Another incident happened when I went online with Hewlett-Packard to fix something that was wrong with my computer, and the agent said I needed an adaptor cord. I ordered it right then and there and it came the next day. We took it out of the box, tried it, and it made absolutely no difference. I called the company back and spoke to between 15 and 20 different agents, just asking for a return label so I could return it. No one could help me, and finally, we figured out that it was Amazon from whom it was ordered, and the agent there finally told me they would cancel the order, I would not have to send it back, and I would not owe anything. Another blessing!

My son Joe then called one day and said his job had ended, and he had all this free time, and would I like him and his wife to come over and help me figure out my finances? How about that as a blessing?

The next blessing came in the form of a Mr. Howard, although his accent was East-Indian, who answered a call on my computer. This one had to go into my computer, and he would be able to fix it when others hadn't, and it was only $299. So I did, and he proceeded to go into my computer with his, and he did fix it. Later a woman from a credit card company called and asked if I had made an order to a certain company, called GCK, and not having recognized the name, I said," No," so she said she would cancel the order, and I would not be responsible for paying it, and my money was returned. Wasn't that a blessing?

And then I remembered! I *had* ordered from that company! So, I tried to call them back, saying, "Is Mr. John Howard there?"

The man said, "No, John is not here; what can I help you with?"

I explained he had fixed my computer remotely, but when the credit card company person asked if I had dealings with the company she mentioned, I said no, I did not recognize it.

He asked, "Did we help you? Did we fix the problem?"

I said, "Yes, he did; it's working now!"

He answered, "Well, if we helped you, and it's working now, then you don't owe us anything!"

How many blessings can one person have?

More than that, yes, more than that. With so many churches losing members and/or closing their doors, especially since

COVID, we are fortunate to have our church still open, although our Mass is on Saturday evening instead of Sunday,and we have a Music Director who plays every week. We are also blessed to have an American priest who is also English-speaking, although we share him with two other churches. We endured three non-English-speaking priests for over twenty years. More blessings: before Covid, we were lucky to have a knowledgeable organist and 14 in the choir. Now we have three singers in the choir, But are we blessed? Yes, we are.

Quiet

Linda Hawley

Turning the TV off sets me free.
A calming stillness comes over me.
Asthma has me listening to my breathing.
It's not bad, there is no wheezing.
Seems there is buzzing in my head,
Just telling me I'm not yet dead.
Hopefully noise is the cat's adventure.
Not a ghost searching for treasure.
Peace has arrived you would agree.
Slowly a sweet calm comes over me.

Cow Pasture

Linda Hawley

In the morning our father would give us kids a ride to "Cow Pasture" which was at the south end of Tamarack Lake. Before the veterinarian, Dr. Rader, built his house at this location, it was a pasture for cows. The name stuck. We were there for swimming lessons with George Goulet. Afterwards our father would come back. "Hey, are you kids ready to go home?"

We would shout back "Yes, we're ready for lunch!" And away we went.

After we ate Kathy, Elaine and I would start our one and a half mile walk down Main Street on our way back to Cow Pasture. Always we would stop at the Stebbins General Store at the corner of Lincoln and Washington Avenues. It smelled different there than other stores. Maybe it's because it had never been remodeled. It probably looked the same in 1900. We would find wax bottles with liquid, Candy Buttons and even red wax lips for treats.

Then we would take a shortcut by walking on the railroad tracks the rest of the way.

Mr. Goulet was there as the lifeguard. After we swam for a while, Mr. Goulet asked "What are you young ladies up to today?"

That day Elaine said "We are playing that we are in a group. My name is Ringo because Ringo Starr is my favorite Beatle." Kathy popped up "My name is Cisco after the Cisco Kid."

I said my name is Poncho. James Franciosa portrayed him on the TV series Valentine's Day." Mr. Goulet said, "I'll be El Cid." Was he planning to be our leader? We all had a fun afternoon.

Principal George Goulet

Learning to Drive in Lakeview

Kathy Nerychel

While I grew up in Saginaw, our family had a summer cottage on Townline Lake. We spent most of the summer at "the Lake." The summer of my 15th year, my mom made a few phone calls, and I was fortunate to be able to take Driver's Training in the village of Lakeview. My cousin, Jeanne and Uncle David also took DT with me, as they too spent summers at the lake. This was back in the days when Driver's Training was part of Community Education and the local school district administered the classes.

My teacher was Mr. Jerry Young, who taught for Lakeview Schools for many years, along with his wife, Natalie. Both he and his wife had polio as children, and as a consequence, he had a distinctive gait and wore a metal brace on his leg that "clicked" it into place when he sat down in the car.

We did several hours of classwork, and finally, we were ready to practice driving. The schedule called for me to drive with a boy named Zeke Quisenberry and another girl whose name I have forgotten for my first session. I was amazed at Zeke's name - it was so unique! One would think with a long last name his parents would've given him an easier first name, but no, his first name was actually Ezekial. It was distinctive, as I remember him now, more than 50 years later. He was a normal looking boy, a farmer, who had been driving tractors and trucks since he could climb up on the seat.

Zeke drove first, doing a fine job on the country roads. He would have no trouble passing this session. Did I mention the sedan we were driving was a stick shift? I was next and took my position behind the wheel. Mr. Young helped me get the vehicle going, and we headed out north of town, towards Cutler (Airport) Rd. I signaled a right turn, and motored down Cutler Road, thinking, "I've got this."

As we neared the end of the road, I knew I would have to turn one way or another. Mr. Young gave me directions on slowing, shifting and turning. My sweaty hands gripped the steering wheel and somehow, inexperienced driver that I was, I turned the wheel too soon, and headed for the wetlands on the north side of the intersection. "Oh no!" We were going to be stuck in the muck of the swamp!

Suddenly I heard the distinctive click and clack of Mr. Young's leg brace. He was swiftly applying the brake from his side of the car. Fortunately, there were no other cars on the road, or there would have been a collision. Of course, the car stalled. Of course, Mr. Young calmly instructed me to put the car in reverse and head back to the

49

blacktop. I was shaken, the backseat passengers were stunned, and Mr. Young looked a bit exasperated.

With my instructor's directions, I quietly turned the corner and soon turned the car over to the next driver. The following sessions were uneventful.

Amazingly, I passed Driver's Training. Maybe Mr. Young just didn't want to work with a crazy, inexperienced girl from Saginaw any longer. Amazingly, my first car was a stick, a big, olive green, tank-like Ford Galaxy. It was my mode of transportation until my sister borrowed it and side-swiped something and I earned enough to buy another, newer car. I remember the price of gas was $.29 a gallon.

Ironically, I grew up, became a proficient driver, and married a good man who lived in Lakeview. We live on Townline Lake and I frequently pass the corner I was almost mired in. I'm sure the tire tracks are gone now. As I drive by the intersection of Bale and Cutler Roads, I think of Mr. Young, who in my opinion, had the ultimate Driver's Training patience.

Four Strong Women

Dorothy May Mercer

The day, hot and sunny,
The task was not funny,
The sand being runny,
T'was costing much money.

So, Dorothy –Great Grammy
And Shelley, the granny
With Mama--sweet Emily
And two-year-old Maddie
These four relations
From four generations
With cheers and elation
Built the foundation.
A sturdy rock wall
To stop the bank's fall
.   Dear God, bless them all!

Country Girl /City Girl

Marian Stockwell

Life just wasn't fair! Why did they get to milk cows, drive tractors, and play in the hay mow, crawling through hay tunnels and swinging on the barn rope? Me, I had to play kickball in a small yard, my pet ducks didn't have much room, and I had to put up with mean pesky neighbors close, right across the street!

City schools weren't as much fun as the country schools, I was sure of it! We walked to school past subdivisions where the houses were so close, they probably could watch their neighbor's television, if the curtains were open. We even had to cross streets so big and busy that there were crossing guards. I'm sure my cousins were riding school buses down neat looking country roads past fields of cows and horses. After school, I'll bet they got to ride their bikes together with friendly, fun neighbors that lived at least a half mile away! Their schools were also much smaller in number of students than the Flint Public Schools. But of course, kindergarten through third grade we were in a one - room building, about the size of a small, manufactured home. In high school, I'll bet they knew everyone in their grade and their siblings' grades as well, probably the whole school even. On the other hand, I didn't even know all the kids in my classes, unless they were nice and cute maybe.

It just wasn't fair, why did my dad move from the comfort of Montcalm County and get a job in Flint of all places! Well, let's see, maybe it was the fact that my mom moved there to go to

Hurley Nursing School located in Flint and was studying to be an RN while my dad was away in the Army, having been drafted. They got married in McBride's Day Bethel Baptist Church one snowstorm in late December. Dad returned to Ft. Benning and mother finished up her nursing program and then joined my dad in Georgia.

But, why couldn't they then go back to their family, their roots? So what if they had twin babies born, mouths to feed and job offers at Hurley Hospital and the motor companies? Why didn't they think about the future life that they were depriving me of, number 4 child? I wanted to live the life of fun, sun, and the fresh air of the country.

When we visited my country cousins, we always had so much fun. I just knew that they were having this much fun every day in Montcalm County, while I was stuck in the city! For example, we rode my cousin Jackie's ponies fast and furious, with only halters. My sister even had the ripped shirt to prove it, as the ponies tried to scrape us off into the trees! Jackie not only had horses, but she and her sisters Vickie and Patsy got to live next door to my grandma for a while. We rode on the back of my cousin Connie's snowmobiles for miles, I'm sure; their little dachshund trying hard to keep up. We had bonfires, hiked on trails in the woods and walked around a lake right across the road from where they lived. They even had an inside archery range, how fun is that, playing Robin Hood, shooting at targets? Even the adults (including my grandma and grandpa)

enjoyed shooting bows, many like my parents, buying their own bows. The inside range also had shuffleboard courts. Wow!

I fell in love with my grandmother Jessie's 1800's hip style barn, upstairs hay mow with the cow stanchions in the lowest floor of the barn. It is so sad to see these majestic pieces of history crumbling in disrepair or empty, not being used. I did eventually get to live in an 1800's old farmhouse that had been renovated (not in Montcalm County) and it had the old 1800's hip style barn with the wooden dowels. My husband and I filled it with horses, a goat, chickens, and barn cats. I finally had my "farmette", with a hay field, pond, and a large garden.

When we were lucky enough to visit the working dairy farms of my aunts and uncles in Montcalm County, it was so exciting, how could it be work? I had cousins in both my mother and father's families that lived on dairy farms. At my Uncle Jim and Aunt Bonnie Ashbaugh's farm we bottle fed the calves that were in their straw pens. I fell in love just looking at their sweet faces and long beautiful eyelashes, I will always remember that. Did my cousins even know how lucky they were to be able to bottle feed calves every day if they wanted to? And what child wouldn't want to?

On my father's side of the family, we watched my cousin Glenn ride one of the cows only after we were sworn to secrecy not to tell his mom or dad! My Uncle Nile let us milk a cow by hand, I loved that. Uncle Nile would squirt milk into the eagerly waiting cats, for our delight, I'm sure. Even barn cats were luckier than us! Harley the bull fascinated us, with a ring through his nose. We knew that bulls were very dangerous and didn't get too close to him at all! My cousin Sheila could ride her horse whenever she wanted. I was sure she dropped her schoolbooks and rode country trails every day after school, while I played kickball with the neighborhood gang!

As an adult, I realize that it probably wasn't fun every day growing up on a farm. It was a lot of work, I'm sure, but rewarding work. As my Aunt Bonnie stated, **"It was a lot of never finished work, dawn to dusk!!!"**

But the kiddos did get a good idea of NEED to work and finish a job, made good foundation for their grownup years." I also am sure that my aunt and uncle are/were very proud of the adults they have become.

I called my cousin Ann Minkel (Ashbaugh), to see if maybe she wished that she lived in the city so that she didn't have to get up before school and do barn chores, and once again in the evening. Maybe it wasn't all that fun, I was just imagining it. But, when we talked, to my surprise, they had even more fun than I had imagined, exploring the woods, ponds, snowmobiling, riding horses and having lots of fun. She visited her cousin in the city during the summer, and talked of how boring that was, after going to the museum and the park, hardly even a backyard. There wasn't a lot else to do compared to down-on-the-farm. Annie and her brothers also did indeed know all of the students in their grade and the whole school even! Not once did she think about switching places with her city cousins, (I wouldn't blame her) and never realized how lucky they were! So much for the theory "The grass is always greener on the other side of the fence".

I am sharing this article and my adolescent years with you to show how my love and fascination with agriculture in Montcalm County grew and developed. This is also why when I was approached with the chance to write a column in the Lakeview Area News about "Our Awesome Agriculture", I was both thrilled and honored.

Morning Person

Kathy Nerychel

In the morning, I have time to get my projects done.
I'm an eager optimist, energized by the sun.
I can do it all, because I have all day.
"Everything's possible if I just get started," I say.

I like to work out with my husband Frank.
Out the door to exercise, him I thank.
Early morning risers with the same habit
Know it's the best time to get it done, just nab it.

We drive back home to fix breakfast.
A healthy start so I have energy to last.
Start my machines, helping me clean:
The dishwasher, dryer and washing machine.

Next check my desk and phone for today's tasks.
Try to do what's important, myself I ask.
The sunshine is streaming through the window.
I take a minute to reflect, and then off I go.

The Garage Across from Imperial

Linda Hawley

In 1962 my sisters, Elaine and Kathy, and I were looking for an exciting place to play. Next to our garage we noticed some piping behind the Imhoff Shop. When we climbed up the piping, we could reach the roof of our garage. Occasionally, we did climb to the peak of the garage to prove our bravery, but we never ventured to the other side of the roof. Falling from that side would land us on cement stairs.

There was a distance of 23 inches between the brick Imhoff Shop and our garage. The three of us were quite happy sitting at the edge of the roof with our feet resting on the Imhoff building. We felt brave to be up there but still safe enough.

Once in a while we would play Tarzan. Other than that, we were content watching people who walked by and listening to what was going on at Imhoffs.

Not long after we started sitting on the roof, we considered having a hideout in the attic of the garage. No one would see us in there. Elaine said "There is a good chance that we could get in trouble. It wouldn't be worth it." We decided not to let that stop us. We found a ladder and went investigating. As far as we could see it was full of filth and junk. And there wasn't much room to even move around. There were at least 13 years of dirt and cobwebs. It was pretty scary.

We did get permission to spend the night up there.

We were petrified of falling off the edge while we were sleeping and got as far from the edge as we could. We brought enough snacks to last the night: packs of wax bottles, Milk Duds, Candy Buttons, Bit-O-Honey and even candy cigarettes. We did survive but never went up there again. We had proved that we had nerve.

We had found a door up there that went to my bedroom. My brother, Ron, and my father got the door down and hung it. I had been the only one in our family with a curtain at my bedroom entrance. Now I was the only one with a real bedroom door.

About 1965 our garage was home to many wooden carved colorful carousel animals. There were goats, camels, lions, horses and even a green sea creature. The most magnificent animal was a large black horse with a curly mane. It was covered with red roses.

Our father speculated "This black beauty had just won the Kentucky Derby and been presented with red roses."

Ours was a special garage!

Jigsaw Puzzles for Brain Improvement

Dorothy May Mercer

One jigsaw puzzle per week is my average. Can anyone or anything interfere with that? Only if we have Sunday company for dinner, or we are out of town. I even take puzzles on vacation.

Every Sunday I open our felt-covered puzzle board and spread it out on our dining room table. I have dozens of puzzles from which to choose—so many that I have forsaken buying any more. And thus, one of my favorite Christmas gifts to receive is a new puzzle. 500 pieces is my upper limit. I don't have the patience or the eyesight for 1000 pieces or more.

Before I turn and sort the pieces, I examine the picture on the box, taking note of certain distinguishing characteristics. It might be a certain figure, or color. Red items are good because red pieces are easy to spot. Another is anything with lines such as a fence, or road. Butterflies are fun and easy to spot, as well.

As I turn and sort the pieces, I choose no more than three or four small piles in addition to the straight edges. A typical sort could be by straight edges, sky, fence, butterfly, and red barn, for example. All the rest of the pieces go into one big pile.

Doesn't everyone start with the edge pieces? Well ... no, not now. I used to start with edge pieces, until I was able to coax my husband to join me. In order to entice him to play with me I did three things. One was to order large-piece, 300-piece puzzles. The second was to make it his job to do the edge pieces. (Call it bribery.) The third is to first turn over and sort all the pieces myself. After a year or more, he has worked up to doing 500-piece puzzles with me. He still gets the edges, first, while I start on other sections. But, after that he will work a bit on the interior of the puzzle. "I found a piece of your puzzle," he might brag on Tuesday or Wednesday.

Unlike many puzzle aficionados, (Note: new word) I like to do the sky first. Why? Because it is all blue—easy to sort—and close to the edge. I've observed that Dave often starts with the sky, and so, by the time he has that done, I will have the blue sky ready to attach to his edge.

Next, I will work on the small piles I have sorted out, one at a time, usually concentrating on items close to the edge first, so I can attach it to Dave's edges. But, depending on the picture, I may have to do a big item in the middle. It could be a horse and carriage, or a building. These types of items are easier than flowers and grass because they have regular lines. Carriage wheels stand out.

How do I look for a particular piece? Once you establish the likely color and/or lines, you need to consider the actual shape of the piece. You eye the hole that it must fill and then somehow your brain translates that to a reverse image. Sometimes you only have one edge, but it is easier if you have two or more. You count the knobs and holes. You might say to yourself: "I'm looking for a piece that has three knobs and one hole. Two of the knobs are white and one is black." Then you begin looking in your pile of white and black pieces. If you find a candidate, you look back and forth from the piece to the spot and compare in your mind, "Will it fit?" If not, you already know why it won't fit, and have, thus, refined your image. Perhaps it is close enough that you pick it up and try it in the spot. Now you know why it doesn't fit, and you add that knowledge to your memory bank. Maybe you need to look for one with longer side, or a slanted knob—whatever.

As you keep trying pieces, your image becomes better and better until suddenly you see "The" piece.

A mistake that Dave makes is his dogged determination to find a particular piece. Not smart. After a certain length of time, it is better to give up and look for another piece. Either that piece is indeed lost, or your idea is all wrong. Much later the correct piece will turn up and you will tell yourself, "Oh that's what that thing looks like." Your idea was all wrong.

Another way that I look is to concentrate on just one characteristic of the piece, rather than trying to visualize the whole piece. If I can imagine just one unusual thing, I can spot it quickly. Maybe it has just one knob and it is unique in some way. It could be a fat knob with a skinny base, or slanted a certain way, or pointed, or the tiniest knob. Maybe it is a large blue knob with a black slanted line across it. Any special characteristic that will be different from every other piece makes it easy to spot. I might find a half dozen blue knobs with a black line across them. That is okay. I pick them all up and try them, one at a time. In trying, I learn more about the missing piece.

There are games to play to sharpen your memory. Once you have the image in your mind of what the piece should look like, test yourself to see how long you can hold that image in your mind without looking back, as you are scanning the loose pieces. An even harder test is to try to look for two different pieces at once. Have you ever moved on to looking for something else, and ten minutes later you suddenly find that piece you were looking for ten minutes ago? I have.

Doing jigsaw puzzles will probably never be Dave's favorite thing. And so, he will lose interest, while I go on working on the puzzle for a few days. When I get close to the end, I may call, "Hey, Dave. You'd better get over here if you want to help finish this puzzle."

And so, he will join me. I divide up the remaining pieces between the two of us, and we take turns finishing the puzzle. My magnanimous (Note: new word) husband will usually insist that I have the honor of putting in the last piece. Or the next to the last piece if one is lost. In that case, the two of us will go on a search, inside the empty box, on the floor, and down inside the chair cushions. Most of our puzzles have all their pieces, but I do have a small jar in which I keep my orphan pieces. Occasionally, we find that missing member and then rejoice.

Finally, we slide the completed puzzle off the felt-covered puzzle board, onto the table, and store the puzzle board and the empty box away for the rest of the week, until it is Sunday—new puzzle day—again.

"New Math"

Linda Hawley

Loved "New Math" in 1961
Mr. Wood made it fun
Even taught our parents at night
They could help us do it right
Addition and division
Can help you make decisions
Decimals and fractions
Can cause distractions
Algebra is where I did excel
Equations I figured out well
I was prepping for success
It surprised me, I do confess

Mr. James Wood

Picking Zucchini

Kathy Nerychel

In the summer of zucchini
I waded into a garden of giant leaves.
Growing together intertwined.
Plants clustered too closely together.
Abundant yellow blossoms promise more squash.
Bees buzzing busily,
Foot-sized leaves touch fuzzily.
Stepping lightly to peer for long green squash
Hiding in the large leaf shade.
Sun shines on their crazy growth.
I grab a big one and escape.

The Give and Take of Phases

Dorothy May Mercer

Bulletin: A strange new disease has inundated the United States, resulting in "shelter in place" orders.

Yesterday, we were presented with good news concerning Phases One, Two, and Three. Presumably, if we Michiganders, as a group, remain sheltered in place a little longer, Michigan could complete the required fourteen days of decreasing numbers and make it to Phase One.

My heart soared until I noticed this footnote: Those in the "Vulnerable" group will stay sheltered until Phase Three, or was it Phase Four? Now confused, a sliver of hope remained until I quickly totaled the weeks. To my sorrow, I concluded that even if all goes well, the "Vulnerables" will have joined the "Deplorables," as outcasts of society, for at least six weeks.

Feeling all alone, today, I was hit with more sad and surprising news from Dr. Oz: Sixty percent of the adult population is in the "Vulnerable" group (which includes the elderly plus anyone with an underlying "health condition"). Really? How can this be? Is it true that only forty percent of the population is able-bodied, i.e., young and healthy enough to go to the beach, the bar, clinic, library, barber shop, etc., driving for pleasure or fishing in their motorboat? Horrors!

Oh well, I guess I'm not so alone after all.

Eighty-three

Gail Shenemen

My big birthday this year was on Labor Day, Monday.
Joe had to be different, he came on Sunday.
He and Sharon brought food and their white dog, Dash.
I had a new cat; he was after the cat in a flash!

I grabbed Ginger and held her up,
To keep her away from that raucous pup.
Joe called the dog off, who was on a line;
He left Ginger alone; the cat was fine.

This morning, I got up and Ginger was Sally
"Boy, Carl," I said, "You don't dally!"
I said that was really strange,
For I was thinking of the same name!

When I was a girl, very small,
My grandmas each gave me a doll.
Katie and Sally were their names.
And now my two dollies are back again.

Randy and Carol called the same day.
They could not come; they were going away.
I had emailed his kids, Randy Jr. and Stephanie
And Darly's daughter, Brittany.

No answer from Randy and Steph,
But Brittany did send a text.
Something came up and she couldn't come;
We received the news when we were done.

Corey came alone, he's single now.
Bethy also arrived without Doug.
Doug didn't come, he doesn't socialize;
He did not know our dessert would be pies.

Jackie, my sister, came without Lou.
He was too busy, what can you do?
Mickey called from Okinawa, can't afford to come home,
Daryl's in heaven, so he's not alone.

So, the five of us feasted on meatballs and rice
And cheesy potatoes, zucchini bread, fruit and pies.
The rest of the family can just stay away,
If they can't come to see me on my birthday.

I Never Would Have Believed This

Gail Shenemen

I was at my hairdresser's, when her colleague came in. She said,:" Hi, Gail; How're you doing?"
I said, "Oh, I'm okay." I was about to tell her about our trip to Branson.

"No," she said. "How are you really doing? Did you go to jail?"

"No, I didn't go to jail; I was in jail when I was 13."

"You were in jail when you were 13?"

"Yes, I was." And I proceeded to tell the story.

We were living in Oregon across the highway from the Columbia River. The Columbia River separates Oregon from Washington. The Dalles is the County Seat and where all government offices are located, and the schools.

We were "squatting" on a piece of property, maybe ten acres, enclosed by three fifty-foot cliffs, through which the train tunnel went east and west. We had our milk goats and bunny rabbits with us. They took shelter in some of the shallow caves in the lower walls of the cliffs. On the north side was the highway, with a pond between the highway and the property.

We were living in a 16x16 surplus army tent with a center pole. Daddy and Mama had bought several old junk cars, which were lying around, outside the tent. They had gone somewhere to look at another one, as they wanted to start a junk yard.

My three sisters had gone on the school bus to school, and I stayed home, which I never did, but I felt sick to my stomach. I was wearing an old, ragged pair of pj's and an old, ragged coat. I had not intended to go out anywhere. It was starting to rain outside.

The wind was always blowing sand and sand was in everything and everywhere. It wasn't long before the wind started whipping up, and the tent started shaking. The wind got stronger, and the rain started pelting everything and the guide ropes for the tent were coming out of the ground. The center pole tipped down; the side flaps were waving around. We had three double beds and a white-gas kitchen stove and a table and chairs. I was afraid the beds would start blowing around, too. I ran outside, because the boxes we had stored inside the tent were blowing out and scattering all over. I tried to grab them and save them. They were blowing into the pond between the tent and the road, where we played in the water when we were home and not in school. This was the beginning of a tornado.

I was running around grabbing papers and other stuff that were being blown all over the yard, which was not a lawn, just tufts of some kind of wild grass, that grew sporadically all over between the cliffs. The papers and other things were spotting the grounds, going farther and farther and into the pond. I was running around like a crazy person, and the old cars that Daddy was collecting to start a junk yard were rolling around over by the cliffs.

I saw a green sedan go west on the highway and then I couldn't pay attention to what was going on out there, because I was trying to save our property.

Suddenly, the same green car was pulling up in the driveway, and it had a gold State Seal on the doors. It must have gone farther west and turned around and came back. I was surprised that he even came there, but a well-dressed official-looking man got out of the car and approached me. He probably showed me his ID; I don't remember. Now, I was old enough to know not to go anywhere with strangers, let alone a lone man, or getting into a strange car. But this car had the State Seal on it.

He said, "What are you doing here? Why are you here alone? Where are your parents? Shouldn't you be in school?"

I answered and told him the situation. He then said, "Well, you can't stay here. This is dangerous. I cannot allow you to stay here alone. I'll have to take you into town to the police."

"The police?" I spoke, my voice shaking, "Why?"

"They will take care of you, and we'll send someone out to let your family know. But you just cannot stay here."

So, in my ragged old pj's and old coat, I got into the backseat of the car, he got into the front, and drove me to the Police Station in The Dalles.

A clerk took me into an office, and made up a record for me, and then she took me into a nice, clean cell, with a single bed, with nice, clean white sheets and pillow (No sand in this bed.) I thought "Wow! I could stay here! For a long time!"

72

They gave me some magazines to read, and there was a good reading light, so I settled in for the night; and a little later, they brought me a tray of supper, which was very good (no sand in that food.)

Then there was a commotion in the hallway, and there was my dad. I knew it was him by the ruckus he was creating in the office. A State Policeman Trooper had come all the way, 10 miles, out there to our 'place' and told Daddy and Mama about the man who came and where he took me and said that I was okay and safe. Daddy yelled at him, "Jesus Christ, Man, why didn't you bring her with you?"

The trooper answered, "I was not allowed to, Sir. You have to go to the jail and sign her out."

So, Daddy got in the truck and came to the police station. He signed me out and the female officer came in with him to take me out.

We got in the truck, and he drove us home. I thought he would be glad that I was safe, and alive, and everything, but all he did was yell at me: "Did you think about how much gas it would cost to come and get you? Why did you let that man take you? Why didn't you stay there? Why didn't you get into one of the old junkers?"

"Are you kidding me? No way! Those old cars were rolling around, too! I would have been blown away, too." I thought. But I didn't say anything; I just burst into tears.

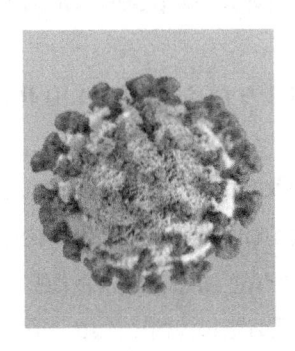

Stay in Quarantine

Raeanna Davidson

Sitting at home in quarantine.
Do not go anywhere. Stay at home in quarantine.
Go to the store when you need food for your family.
Just hope that this will go away soon.

But what can we do?
Staying at home is no fun.
To stay at home every day and all day long.

So stay home and be safe, that's all we can do.

Anticipating a Storm

Linda Hawley

Hoping electricity won't go off
Situation would not help my cough
At my left hand is my flashlight
A lantern at my right
Phone is fully charged
My ego is enlarged
I'm at peace in my soul
Have it all under control

Daddy Back

Kathy Nerychel

We arrived in Atlanta at 7:57 a.m. The Atlanta airport is a great place to people watch, as it is a major hub in the U.S. Travelers from everywhere are coming and going. Atlanta has two terminals, Domestic and International Travel, as well as five concourses, labeled A, B, C, D & E. Sometimes you need to take a train, elevator, or escalator to make your connecting flight. There are 34 gates on the A concourse, where we are transferring to our Delta flight to St. Thomas.

A bare-midriffed girl in capris and flip flops walking contrasts with a young lady striding quickly in the opposite direction in a long winter coat, boots, and a knit hat with a poofy pompom on top. Everyone is going somewhere, except for the folks who work here- and that's a pretty big group of people too. Some are from warm environments, some from colder places.

Also surging past are groups of service men and women. Three sailors walked by just now, and I am proud to see them. They get deferential treatment boarding the plane and at the various shops. The sailors are seated in the area for a flight to Miami. That makes sense. The young National Guard ladies and gentlemen seem to prefer Chick-Fil-A.

As we wait for our flight to board, a story unfolds in the theater of the concourse in front of us. A young mother with three little ones, two toddler boys and a baby girl in arms, a stroller, and a large sign, rolls over to the stainless-steel post near our seats at the boarding/disembarking area by us, Gate # 12. She tells the two little boys, "Stand by the post with the stroller." While she shifts the little one to her other hip.
I notice their t-shirts, which say, "Stay out of my way, I get my daddy back today."

All three kiddos have matching grey t-shirts with that sentence, even the baby. Mom hands the tallest toddler the sign, which is almost as big as he is. He turns it upside down and then puts it on his head. Mom, holding baby sister precariously, helps him turn the sign around. It says, "Welcome Home Daddy."

Then they wait, as patiently as three little ones can wait. Those of us witnessing this drama, watch the passengers begin to file off the plane, trying to guess which gentleman is their daddy.

"Look for Daddy," mom admonishes the boys, as they turn the sign this way and that, and set it on the ground. Passengers walking off the plane smile at the cute kids waiting for daddy.

When their father strides off the plane, he is grinning broadly and very tall, perhaps 6 feet 7 or 8. He is wearing boots and a large khaki knapsack that says, "USDA." He kneels on one knee and gathers the two boys into his arms for a huge hug, while Mom takes a picture with her phone. Then he kisses mom and baby sister, too.

Next mom transfers the littlest one to her dad, and he kneels with the three children encircled in his arms. Mom clicks on another photo. A traveler steps up and offers to take a picture of the whole family. Mom poses with Dad - she hardly reaches his shoulder, and the cuties in t-shirts. They thank the stranger, gather up the sign, stroller and toddlers and head for home.

We were fortunate to share a heartfelt homecoming with a sweet family at Gate #12. Those of us seated nearby smiled imagining Daddy's homecoming.

I Cry Out

Raeanna Davidson

I cried out, and you were not there.
I tried, and you did not care.
I was here, and you left me.
I wish things could be different.

But you will always be the same.
I will cry out, and you will not hear me.
It is like you don't care about me.
Sometimes I wish you weren't in heaven.

Sometimes when I am here, you are not.
My heart is hurting; I feel like crying,
Because you are not here
.I felt sad when I lost you, still to this day.

I wonder if you can hear me cry out to you.
Do you hear me asking you why did you go?
But no matter what, I will always love you
From this moment on. God bless you on this day.

Two Religious Experiences on St. Thomas

Kathy Nerychel

Our new friends, Mike and Barb, from Naples, Florida, had spent a day exploring downtown Charlotte Amalie, the harbor town. They gave us suggestions for historic places to visit. They said we must check out the fort, climb the historic 99 steps and visit St. Thomas, the Jewish synagogue.

The fort was painted red, and the walls were three feet thick. Built in 1671 by the Danish king, it is now a museum. When we toured it, we found dungeons in the cement-walled basement which contrasted with the governor's sections of the building. The governor's quarters featured lovely mahogany furniture and hand-painted China. There were secret passageways that were fun to explore. Up on the roof, the panoramic view included cooling ocean breezes and a bird's eye view of the town, the harbor and up the mountain.

Our route downtown passed through an open-air marketplace where we did a bit of shopping. We turned inland and climbed 99 ancient steps (I think there were more than that!) Built by the Danish, they were designed to solve the problem of getting around the hilly terrain, The bricks in the steps were transported from Denmark. The Governor's current house was parallel to the top stairs and was constructed between 1865 and 1867. It was a large white columned mansion, guarded by colorfully costumed soldiers. We took photos on the lanai.

After consulting our map and GPS, we turned east towards the second oldest synagogue in the Western Hemisphere. It is known for the white sand floor, which is kept commemorating the exodus of the Jews from Egypt. The tracks of Jews through the sand could be obliterated, and they couldn't be followed. We took a tour of the building with a docent named Rob. He gave us the history of the Jewish exploration of the Virgin Islands in response to their persecution in Spain. The Spanish killed Jews who refused to become Christians, and many of them joined the ships searching for a passage to the West Indies in the 1400s. Today, their new rabbi, a female, joins their congregation from Africa.   Finally, our guide told us about the torahs, the sacred scrolls of this Jewish congregation. One torah was originally from Czechoslovakia but had been stolen by Hitler during World War II along with other religious items and art work and kept in warehouses. The Jews were persecuted by the Nazis and confined to concentration camps, but after the war, the artifacts were restored to churches and synagogues. The St. Thomas Jewish congregation was fortuitously able to obtain this meaningful torah. My husband's father's family

81

came from Czechoslovakia, so he was very intrigued by this history. I was touched by the perspective on history from a Jewish point of view.

After stopping by the congregation's gift shop, we headed downhill for lunch and then back to our room. But the memory of this stop on our journey has stayed in our minds and hearts.

*****

On Saturday of the same week, we said good-bye to our two-week home in St. Thomas. We turned in our rental car at the airport, and arrived four hours early, to allow time to process through security and customs. After gathering our belongings and putting on our shoes, we joined a large crowd of people awaiting a flight off the island. The airport terminal was not designed to hold as many people as were there. There were food kiosks, duty-free shops, restrooms and one café. We decided to eat, as it was after noon, and I tried "salty fish Pate" which I found to be very fishy and salty. We made a couple trips around the crowded terminal, carrying our food, pulling our luggage, looking for two seats to sit and eat. Finally, Frank spied one empty seat and the lady next to it offered us her spot. We took it!

As we ate lunch, the traveler next to Frank stood up and left. An African American gentleman with a priest's white collar sat down next to Frank. Both of us ate and conversed with the people on either side of us. Frank talked to the priest, who said his flight to Philadelphia had been delayed and changed twice. He was flying to Harrisburg to speak on Black History Month on Sunday morning, and to a teen group later Sunday afternoon. He hoped he would make it on time. Frank and he continued their conversation throughout our wait, as the priest checked his ticket changes. Frank, who is not Catholic, nor a churchgoer, enjoyed his discussions with the priest on a variety of topics. Later, we learned that many flights that day had been cancelled or diverted because of a Chinese spy balloon that was spotted off the coast of the Carolinas. No wonder the terminal was so crowded!

I grew warm during our wait, as I was wearing a long-sleeved shirt and blue jeans in the crowded, 80-degree room. I anticipated we would return to snow and cold Michigan weather. Finally, after a long afternoon, our flight was announced. We were boarding!

We said "good-bye" to our seat neighbors, now familiar friends, and the priest next to Frank mentioned that he would give us his blessing.

"I hope you are blessed with a short wait and safe travels, too, Father." I replied.

"Bless you both," the clergyman murmured, making the sign of the cross.

"Thank you, Father." I replied.

"Actually, I'm the bishop of the Virgin Islands." the clergyman told us.

I was astonished that we had shared time with the bishop, and he had given us his blessing. We hoped he would have safe travels on his journey, sharing his experiences of the islands and their people.

Empty Nest – Full Heart

Gail Shenemen

This used to be a busy place
With children running all over the house.
Now that they've all gone away
The house is quiet as a mouse.

I miss them all so very much
But they don't even seem to care.
I see shadows in the hall,
Children lurking everywhere.

And then I realize that they
Are only shadows on the wall.
I was glad when they all grew up
And no longer needed my care.

But I get depressed when I think
Of all the memories nestled there.
I look at photos of the times
That they were living here with me.

I think of all of them
All together and separately.
I was glad when they each one
Started their own family.

But they don't visit anymore.
I guess they must be mad at me.
Then the great-grandchildren come along;
You'd think they'd bring them over.

But do they? No, they don't.
They forget I am the grandmother!
Now our cats have become our kids;
They love us and we love them.

Advice

Illustration by Kim Bunch

Spice of Life

Marian Stockwell

What makes us jump out of bed in the morning thinking or yelling, "Whoopee, today I get to..."

Let's be real, for some of us it may be, "What can tempt me to even get out of bed in the morning?!"

So, let's just imagine that there could be an awesome reason to be excited upon awakening, what would it be? Why is it important to ask ourselves this? Humans can sometimes be creatures of habit, as they say. Humans can fall into the same ol' rut, and then wonder why they feel so depressed, tired, and sick. I believe that there is a direct link between mental well-being and physical well-being.

Am I trying to say that nobody would be sick if they were always happy, bubbly laid back all the time? No, for one thing, very few people are all of the above all of the time. But, of those who are most of the time, it would be interesting to compare the statistics of how many have grave illnesses versus those who are always depressed, in a bad mood, anxiety-ridden and uptight. Some of us may appear happy-go-lucky on the outside, which often I may appear to be, but the reality is, I was called a "worry wart" when I was young as well as being painfully shy. It takes work to counterbalance that personality, let me tell you!

Back to the Spice of Life, does it have to be a trip to Paris, or a new Cadillac, or being engaged to the most gorgeous person? No. How about a movie that we have been waiting to see, because of Covid, we may have even been waiting more than a year; maybe it would be if we get up early, get the jobs done for the day, and then we can go spend the afternoon at the beach. An invitation to somewhere fun is always nice, whether we are invited or doing the inviting. Be creative, think outside the box, and think small and inexpensive if time or money is an issue. Sometimes those events turn out to be the most fun, the most memorable anyway.

At what age do children lose their curiosity, their love of adventure and exploring? Take some time to watch children playing on their own in a park for instance, or in their bedrooms. They have such great imaginations and joy in just the simplest things. Might we be able to regain some of that? Time flies by and the next thing we know we are old! What will we remember and think about when we are rocking on our porch in old age? Will we be thinking back on all the hours spent working or sleeping? Find something to fill that void, to make it worthy of the minutes that we have spent on earth! Make it spectacular!

What does spice look like, and taste like? Let's look at it in food. It is full of different colors, dark reds, clay reds, yellows, white, and black. Oh, the tastes, such a wide variety: from blister the lips and tongue; to cravings for vanilla and cinnamon in coffee; then to the basic earth taste of garlic. My, my what choices right there at our fingertips, meant and put on this earth to give us pleasure. We should be so blessed; enjoy it all!

Spice in our daily life, is it lacking? Well, let's take it up a notch, go out of our comfort zone just a little, and peek around. That's better, isn't it? Does it have to be every day? No, but aim for most days. If we can't fully participate in it, let's live it vicariously through others. For example, if we love golf and are great golfers, we miss it, but now it is just a bit too demanding. Our cookbook says to add that spice called golf back into our lives. What could that look like? Riding in the golf cart on a beautiful day with our favorite golf partner. Offer to keep score and we may be able to throw in some "advice" along the way.

Were we avid runners? At this time, we may not be strong enough to run even a 5 K. Don't be left behind, become a volunteer, hand out water bottles, T-shirts, prizes, etc. Get right in the middle of it all, it is good for the soul and will keep the depression of missing all our friends at the annual events. How about kayaking or just being on the water? Is it a bit too physical currently? How about talking our buddies into a tow, yes that is right, whether in a kayak or maybe on a tube on a shorter excursion. The sun on our faces, our fingers making swirling patterns in the water, sipping on that pina colada, ok, it is a cold fruit drink, but our minds can add that extra spice and make it into a pina colada, or maybe it is just a cold freshly squeezed fruit drink. Still, our minds can add that extra spice and turn it into your drink of choice!

Then there are those days, the ones when it's difficult to get up and get moving. Those days are perfect for a hot mug of coffee or tea while sitting in our favorite, comfy chair where we can go on an exciting, romantic adventure or journey through a book, whether held in our hands or on our Kindle. What about creating and letting our imagination roam, whether through writing poetry or painting? Don't worry so much about the end product, it doesn't have to be a Robert Frost poem or a Picasso painting. It is the enjoyment of the journey that is most important. What about joining a writer's group or taking a class in painting? I participate in a Writer's Group both in Michigan and in Florida. Comments such as, from Jake, "Writer's Group is the highlight of my week, I look forward to it." Or another statement from Jim, "I get so much out of this group, you all inspire me."

The Spice of Life is about finding the donut hole and filling it!

New Hope

Linda Hawley

Once you give up
Fill a coffee cup
Reverse your path
Recalculate the math
Turn your life around
So you don't drown

Be full of hope
Learn to cope
Walk on the positive side
Be full of pride
Learn to love YOU
Start being true blue

The Gift for Me

Charleen Stroup

I didn't know that I had died
When he handed me a gift.
I asked him, "Tell me what's inside?"
The lid was hard to lift.

"Is it my earthly stuff like clothes,
My money and my worth?"
"Oh no," he said, "It's none of those
For they belong to earth."

"Is it the memories in my mind?
For those I'd want to save."
"No, those are of another time,
And stay within the grave."

"It must be talent, music, art,
The things I do so well."
"No, those stay with your earth-bound heart,
That's only where they dwell."

"Okay, my friends and family then,
For they are dear to me."
"No, that's your path, that's where you've been,
Your fleeting jubilee."

He said, "Those things, your body too,
Are not what you will need."
"How about my soul?" My thoughts are through
With guesses of this deed.

"Your soul belongs to me, my friend,
It's not a paradox.
So, go ahead and try again
To open up your box."

I found it empty. I felt faint.
"So, what was mine?" I asked.
"Each loving moment sans complaint,
Good thoughts and deeds you cast.

"The only things that ever last
Beyond a life, my dear,
Are moments, not what's in your past
Nor future thoughts of fear.

"The content of each moment flows
So fast; stand still and feel
Your present moment, it's all you know.
The rest is just unreal."

Math or Arithmetic?
Gail Sheneman'

I think everyone should learn arithmetic or math.
Just to set them on the right path.
To add, subtract, multiply, and divide,
Might not make you the world's best guide.

But these are the basic tools you will use
To live most any life you would choose.
I learned my times tables in third grade up to twenty.
After that I really didn't need plenty.

When we started in fourth grade with "fractions,"
I thought they were wrong; told Mama they meant "factions."
I heard early-on, Hell was made of story problems,
Fraught with vampires, witches, and ghosts and goblins.

I took first-year Algebra, was two months late starting,
But caught up with the class, excelled, it was a party.
Thought I'd never need higher math, and I never did.
I do most problems in my head, no need for calculus or trig.

 I don't use calculators, I need paper for my math,
Especially when I'm doing drafting or a graph.
But I'm almost 85 now and the most math I'll still ever need,
Is to know how fast I'm going, so I can regulate my speed!

I Promise You

Gail Sheneman

I cannot promise you a life without tears.

But I will try to protect you from all fears.

I cannot promise you a life full of joy.

But I will promise to try not to annoy.

My heart is so full of dreams spent with you.

We trust each other with hearts sweet and true.

I cannot give you the stars up above,

And I will not give you a life without love.

Pets

Esmeralda

Linda Hawley

Esmeralda is my name
Ready for any game
Paws catching a bird
You can take my word
Running after a mouse
In this nice big house
There are places to hide
Look behind and inside
Thinking about supper
Please no more blubber
I'm orange, black and white
A right beautiful sight

The New Kitty

Gail Shenemen

Raeanna and her sister-in-law
Brought the best birthday present you ever saw
A calico kitten a few months old
They didn't have room for her in their fold.

Her name was Maria when she came,
But Carl wanted a different name.
He named her "Ginger" because of her color.
It's black and gray stripes and orangy "yeller."

She's a sweet little thing who likes to hide.
"Cuz the other three cats want her outside.
They're very jealous about their place;
They forget they each were once that new face

We love her already and she can sleep on our bed.
If we can ever find where she's hidden.
Then in the morning when we got up
There was Ginger eating from a cup.

She was friendly and nice and sweet as could be
Then Carl decided to call her Sally.
We don't dare let her go outside.
Because Tom Cats are prowling to be satisfied.

But she is too young to have kittens I say
So to the vet to have her spayed
As soon as she is old enough.
But to keep her away from them is tough.

So we'll keep an eye on our Sally
The prettiest calico cat in the valle

Herding Cats

Kathy Nerychel

Mom started feeding a stray gray cat her table scraps. She threw leftovers in the field next to the garage. The cat ate everything she put out, and sometimes brought a friend. We discussed where the kitty came from. Did it belong to the farmer across the road? Was it one of the neighbors? Or just a stray?

Soon, someone bought Mom a bag of cat food, for the days she didn't have leftovers. The cat looked well fed - or was it pregnant?

My sister, Jenny, fixed up a nice plastic tote with a door and soon, there were four kittens running around, eating with the mother cat. As winter drew near, Jenny reinforced the tote with straw to keep the kittens warm. Better get another bag of cat food.

Finally, Mom decided she had too many cats! She didn't want a pet cat! And certainly not five of them! She talked about it with the family, and Susan and Ben, who have a farm and three kitty-loving children, volunteered to take a kitten or two. The date for kitten removal was set.

Coincidently, the day for moving the kittens was the same day my brother, Don and his wife, Deb were mowing Mom's lawn. Another brother, Paul and his wife Cheri, also animal lovers, were there for the kitten round up too. The kittens were nowhere to be seen. Were they afraid of the lawnmower? Or did they know they were being hunted? Oh no! The cats were hiding under the house and the porch.

Everyone pitched in to herd the kittens into baskets and boxes. The cats were frightened and hissing. Somehow, they managed to herd the cats out from under the porch. It was time-consuming and hilarious!

Finally, each of Ben and Susan's children ended up with their favorite kitten. Mom was happy to have the kitten population reduced, and everyone had a story to tell.

But wait! Is Momma Cat getting fat again? Would anyone like a kitten for Christmas?

Kitty

Linda Hawley

Kitty is out there
Breathing sweet fresh air
Escaped from back door
Went out to explore
She is on an adventure
Out there for pleasure
Looking for mice and birds
Not listening to my words
Concerned about fleas
Come back here, please
A cat might bite her
Then she wouldn't purr
Dead by raccoon
Maybe this afternoon
I will sit and wait
She won't be too late
Waiting hour after hour
Now - into candlepower
I am going into limbo
Scratch at the window
Great - now I can go to bed
Kitty is not dead

Cat # 2

Gail Shenemen

The reason the cat peed on my bed
Was Joe brought his dog after I said,
"Don't bring your dog, the cats don't like him.
If he gets too close, the cats will fight him;
They'll tear the fur right off his head;
He'll soon wish that he was dead."

See, there's no litter box in the bedroom
where they hide out when he's here
They have to pass by the family room,
Filled with lots of dread and fear,
Where he is with Sharon and Joe
To get to the laundry room so they can go.

We can hear them growling low
Under the Christmas tree in the living room
Where the dog dares not go,
He barks now, hoping he can scare them
Then all gets quiet as they leave.
Wagging his tail behind him.

Live Like You're Not

Gail Sheneman

How would you like to live like you're not,
And have a different body than you've got?

How would you like to live like a cat?
Just sitting around, eating, and get fat?
Oh, wait! I already do that!
Or run through the woods.
Not eating much food
And not coming home when you should.

Or how about being a goldfish?
Swimming around in a great big dish?
I'm almost sure this would be my wish.
Then they yell, "We want out, to sleep in a bed!"
But they don't know if I do what they said,
Without water they'd all be dead!

What I'd really like to be is a bird,
To fly all over and hear my songs heard.
It wouldn't matter if I couldn't say a word.
To fly, to fly, to float on the air
Just to float all around and go everywhere.
Just to fly like a bird without any care.

Gifts

Linda Hawley

Esmeralda leaves gifts for me
Thoughtful of her you would agree
In morning, outside my bedroom door
Red stuffed cardinal on the floor
She may leave it at her cat bed
Or the recliner, if so led
Returning home was once surprised
At a roll of Charmin as advertised
Then there are things I clean up quick
When she leaves something from being sick
She topped it all Friday, this sweet cat
At the recliner was a dead bat.

Fiction

Vittorio: Messages in my head

Tom Colburn

"Santhi, my beautiful baby girl, my raison d'etre. You don't think I'm crazy, huh?" Vittorio Benson, Vito to his friends, pleaded with his youngest child to validate his sanity.

"Of course not, Papa," she replied. "A little eccentric maybe, but crazy? No, never."

Antonio, Vito's best friend for over 50 years, wasn't so sure.

"Yes, because every *not crazy* person talks to spirit beings who give him great wisdom and revelations."

He rolled his eyes and shook his head.

"Uffa!" he added for emphasis. *Ugh!*

Santhi came to her father's defense.

"Many people in the Bible received visions from angels and even from God himself," she pointed out. "If we believe the Bible, how can we say it's not possible? You're a good

"Yes, of course I believe," Antonio replied. "As God is my witness. But Santhi, my dear girl, I love you like you were my own child, and I love your papa too, he is like a brother to me, but he speaks crazy talk. People will think he's pazzo, nuts! You have to talk some sense into him before he gets locked in a loony bin."

Antonio was laughing but he was only half kidding.

"Lock me up? Why?" Vito protested. "I'm not sacrificing the neighbors' pets to the spirit gods. I'm simply telling you what I saw and heard. I give you honesty. Is that crazy now? You're supposed to be my friend, Antonio. Show a little support, already."

"I am your friend," Antonio countered. "For 50 years I've been your *best* friend. And it's because I'm your friend that I'm begging you to stop this crazy talk. The Vito part of you is paisano. So, this talk must be coming from the Benson half of your brain!"

Antonio was proud of his heritage. His blood was 100% Italiano. He was first generation American. He was proud of that too. He grew up in a household that spoke much more Italian than English and all these years later he still had a hint of an accent. Sometimes he cranked it up a notch for effect.

Vito grew up differently. His mother was first generation Italian. Her dad traced his paternal ancestry to England. English was the only language spoken in Vito's home growing up. His first name was a hat tip to his maternal grandfather, a man the elder Benson admired greatly.

"Maybe we ask Yosef," Vito suggested. "He's a good student of the Hebrew Bible. Maybe he won't be so fast to write off what I say as crazy talk."

Antonio raised his brow doubtfully.

"It's not what you say that I find crazy, Vito," he corrected. "It's where you say the words came from. If someone says they were abducted, flown to some unknown place, and had bad things done to them, I don't doubt that. But when they say it was on an alien spaceship and they were probed by little green creatures, now I think maybe there was some vino involved. Like a few bottles."

"When did I talk of little green creatures, or spaceships, or probing or being transported anywhere?" Vito questioned. "I'm in my own house. I'm minding my own business. Sometimes maybe I'm sipping a glass of vino. Sometimes water or coffee. It's not the drink, Antonio. It's a message. It comes when it comes." "You're not a young man anymore, Vito," Antonio pointed out. "Next year we both turn 65. We're senior citizens. And sometimes, when people get older, maybe we don't think so clearly anymore."

Vito shook his head affirmatively but with a facial expression decidedly cynical.

"Oh, so now I have dementia, you think," Vito mocked. "You don't understand what's happening so I must be crazy. It couldn't possibly be that the great Antonio has stumbled upon something real he's never seen before."

Antonio tossed his hands in the air.

"Ah, we'll talk with Yosef," he replied. "He'll agree with me. You'll see. He'll want to help you too. He is our friend."

"A friend you say you are," Vito remarked sarcastically. "You give me a choice between a muzzle or a mental hospital. Everyone should have such friends. What a happy place the world would be."

He turned toward his daughter before continuing. "What do you think, Santhi? Do you want friends like that? Maybe someday Isabella will be such a good friend like that to you."

Isabella was Antonio's daughter and one of Santhi's two best friends. The other was Talya, Yosef's daughter. All three grew up together, graduated high school together and were now in their senior year of college, the same college, Jefferson Independence, a four-year liberal arts institution that prided itself on accepting no government funds, so they were free to teach according to their own priorities. And teach to their beliefs, they did.

"Issy already thinks I'm crazy," Santhi replied. "And she loves me anyway. If I got sent to a nuthouse, she and Talya would find a way to join me."

The two men laughed knowingly. "I don't doubt that for a minute," Antonio remarked. "How about you, Vito?"

"Not at all," he replied. "These girls are like three strands in a braid."

"Talya and Issy are coming over after supper to study and hang out," Santhi announced. "Maybe the fathers can come over as well and do their amateur shrink session on you, Papa. Who knows, the girls and I might even leave you old guys some wine. Speaking of which, I think I'd like a glass now."

She winked at her father and headed to the kitchen.

"Just a small glass, Santhi," Vito said. "It's still early."

He turned to his friend with a half-smile, shaking his head in mock frustration. "Kids," he said simply.

"I feel your pain," Antonio replied. "Why did we wait until our forties to have these beautiful sassy daughters? What the hell were we doing in our twenties when we should have had them?"

Vito smiled knowingly.

"We were being young and sassy like them," he rejoined.

They shared a laugh.

"Alright. I'll see you tonight then," Antonio said. "With Yosef, if I can talk him into it."

Antonio left and Vito went into the kitchen to make sure Santhi wasn't overdoing it on the wine. She'd turned 21 that year and was taking advantage of her ability to purchase alcohol. She was a responsible girl and hadn't done anything stupid with her new liberty yet—at least that he knew of—but she was still young.

When he entered the room and spotted her at the kitchen table, she was sipping a stiff glass of spring water and sporting a mischievous grin.

"I thought I'd start with something light then work my way up to the good stuff," she said, barely stifling a laugh.

Vito sighed, but not sadly.

"Antonio thinks I'm headed toward crazyville, and now you're trying to give me a push," he complained in jest. "It's a conspiracy!"

He smiled when he said it.

"I don't think you're crazy, Papa, I'm just not really sure what it is you're experiencing. I have time. Can you tell me about it? I promise not to try and shrink you."

"I appreciate that," he said with a grin. "It really kind of snuck up on me one day out of the blue."

"What did?" she inquired.

"The weird messages," he replied. "I mean I'm okay with weird. You know I've always been a little unorthodox in my Christian views."

"Yeah, even when you were still pastoring and all the more so since," she acknowledged. "It has my boyfriend pretty concerned. You know, for your soul."

"Are you concerned as well?" he asked.

"No, because it's pretty obvious you're sincerely searching for the truth," she said. "You want to know. You still have faith. How could any loving God punish you for that?"

"God wouldn't, but doctrines do," Vito replied.

"And there it is," Santhi said. "That right there is what makes Bobby's head spin around like the kid in that old creepy devil movie."

"You mean Linda Blair in the Exorcist?" he asked.

"Yeah, that one. I told him that's not a good look for someone contemplating entering the ministry."

Vito smiled.

"If you two end up marrying we're going to have some interesting conversations at family gatherings, I think," he suggested.

"We do now," she pointed out. "But he better be respectful, or I'll kick him to the curb. I already told him that."

"That's my girl," Vito said smiling proudly, even though he knew she was kidding. Or thought she was.

"So, I was just sitting in the living room on my recliner with Slowboat..."

"My dog?" she asked, surprised.

"Yeah, *your* dog who thinks *my* lap is his home," Vito bemoaned. "This, the most unmotivated creature God ever created, suddenly stopped his snoring, drooling and occasional releasing of one of his toxic surprises, then lifted his floppy-eared, face-drooping head and get this, *barked!*"

"Slowboat barked?" she asked, surprised. "What did you do, spill hot coffee on him?"

"No, I did that once," Vito admitted. "He just shivered briefly, craned his head to give the burned area a few licks, then went back to sleep. No brain, no pain, I guess."

"Poor Slowboat," Santhi said. "He's a basset hound. He's supposed to be a lazy lump. Anyway, what made him bark?"

"I didn't know at first," Vito replied. "I didn't hear anything or see anything. But he obviously did. And then I did too. He was looking right at it. It was a very faint image. Kind of like a hologram in dot matrix if that makes sense."

"Not really, but go on," she said.

"It was just there, suspended in the air. It didn't really look like a person, but maybe an abstract art version of one. Then suddenly, I had this thought in my head. There wasn't any word by word, sentence by sentence communication. I didn't actually *hear* anything. I just instantly knew this message—I guess that's what it was—all at once. Then poof, the mirage or whatever it was, was gone, but the message lingered."

"What was the message?" Santhi inquired.

"It was just two lines," Vito explained. "*All doctrine is of man. Truth is intuitive.*"

"That could have come from your own brain," Santhi pointed out. "It's pretty much what you've said you believe."

"I thought the same thing at first," he revealed. "I thought my brain just gathered my beliefs and summed it up in a concise, somewhat profound two sentence declaration."

"Sounds rational to me," Santhi said. "But you said *at first*. What did you mean?"

"Well, there was one thing that didn't add up," he replied. "Slowboat. He clearly saw what I saw. And he saw it first."

"Maybe it was just a coincidence," she suggested. "Maybe something explainable stirred him up and it just happened to be at the moment of your brain popping that thought into your consciousness."

"Have you met him?" he asked facetiously. "A Cessna flying into the side of the house wouldn't stir that mutt. Something very unusual, something silent and almost invisible, woke him from a dead sleep and made him bark. I mean, how could he see my hallucination if that's what it was?"

"So, you're saying Slowboat's a ghost whisperer?" she joked.

"He must have sensed something that alarmed him while he was still snoring," Vito explained. "Unless maybe whatever that thing communicated, at an audible level it was a sound only a dog could hear. So instead of hearing it I just got the message implanted in my consciousness."

"That is pretty strange, Papa," Santhi conceded. "But it's a one-time thing so maybe Antonio is right. Maybe it's best just to blow it off as some weird trick your brain played on you and forget about it."

"I could and probably would do just that except for one thing," Vito replied.

"Slowboat's reaction?" she asked.

"No, not that," he said. "At least not just that."

"What then?" she inquired.

"I can't blow it off because it wasn't just a one-time thing," he explained. "It's happened two more times since then. Once more with Slowboat, and once alone."

"Did Slowboat respond the same way the second time?" she asked.

"Exactly the same way," he confirmed.

"What were the other messages?" she questioned.

"The second message was, I am one, but I've been many. And the last one was, Your realm came from mine."

"Well, that's not creepy at all," Santhi commented. "What does it all mean?"

"I don't know for sure," he admitted. "All I can figure is either someone is pranking me and Slowboat, or I'm actually getting contacted by beings from another realm. There's only one other possibility I can think of."

"What's that?" she asked.

"That Antonio's right. I'm going crazy."

Tom

Originally from New Hampshire, Tom Colburn moved to Michigan in 2003 and now calls it home. He draws on a lifetime of experience (father of five daughters, retired pastor, U.S. Navy veteran, missionary work in the Far East, former state representative, etc.) to build the fictitious characters and scenarios of his eight novels. He's also published three non-fiction books. Writing is his hobby and passion. Tom Colburn is a retired pastor and has written 17 books.

Sunday Dinner with Sharon

Dorothy May Mercer

Excerpt from Chapter 49

"Pastor B and the Haunted Church"

© 2023 Dorothy May Mercer

Sunday dinner with Sharon was a priority tradition for Rev. Alan. Sometimes they would cook together at home, and sometimes they would go out to a restaurant. They seldom accept invitations on this day of the week. It was a time to relax and catch up with each other.

On this occasion, they had reserved a quiet corner table in one of their favorite places, hoping to avoid people and concentrate on each other. It didn't work out well. Robert Kramer's interview had opened interest in the black history of the church, followed by Phyllis Tiller's interview with Alan that had spawned several network reports. And now, Gene Dillinger's appearance has lit up social media. Alan had to be nice to people who came up to speak to him. Finally, the manager approached their table. "Hello," he said. "I'm the manager here. I'm so sorry you are being bothered."

"Not at all," said Alan graciously.

"Well, actually, we were hoping for a chance to visit," said Sharon. "We haven't seen each other much all week."

"Kindly, let me offer one of our private rooms," he said.

"Oh, I would love that!" Sharon was enthused. Alan was a little embarrassed, but he wisely kept quiet.

"All right, then. Come with me. I think you will enjoy this place." The manager offered his arm.

Soon, Alan and Sharon were seated in a charming private dining room, with soft music, candlelight, comfy chairs, a blazing fireplace, artwork on the walls, a personal waiter, and a view of the garden.

"Enjoy your meal," said the manager.

Sharon looked around and sighed. "Well, what do you think? Isn't this beautiful, Alan?" She knew she had embarrassed him.

"I admit, you were right, Sharon. This is so nice."

The waiter hovered over them, filling their ice water, pouring coffee, offering condiments and a basket of hot rolls. They picked up elegant menus, chose their meals, and placed an order. The waiter quietly vanished.

Alan reached across the table and took Sharon's hand. "You are so beautiful, and I love you dearly."

"I love you, too." She smiled and squeezed his hand.

"Tell me about your book. I haven't had a chance to ask." Alan selected a hot roll.

"Well, sweetheart, you won't believe what I have learned." Sharon used her spoon to fish an ice cube out of her water glass and put it into her hot coffee.

"Tell me," Alan invited, dividing the roll into pieces.

"Ebenezer's library has been a treasure trove of facts and personal stories all about the early church before and after the fire." She stirred her coffee.

"No kidding? I had no idea." Alan spread butter on his hot roll. "I found a detailed list of the early members, their names, families, lives and deaths. Also--get this--a record of every slave that passed through."

"Oh my goodness!" Alan watched the butter melt and savored his first bite.

Sharon's continuous dieting did not allow her to indulge in rolls. "C'mon, take just one bite," Alan teased. "This is so good."

"Well, okay, just one tiny bite," she succumbed.

Alan lavished one piece with butter, "Open," he commanded, and shoved it into her mouth. "Mm, ambrosia," she said as she chewed the overly large piece, swallowed, and reached for her coffee.

Alan smiled. "I told you so," he allowed.

"Well, as I was saying," Sharon sipped while continuing. "Sometimes it would just be a first name, because not everyone had two names. But there would be as many facts as were known. It could be their age, height, weight, families, where they were from in Africa, if they knew, the plantation where they were enslaved, how long they were on the road, and where they hoped to go. The date and time they arrived and left. Sometimes there would be a short narrative about them. It was fascinating."

"Have you put that all in your book?"

"Oh yes, I have an indexed list of all the names and facts. In some cases, it is cross-indexed because other family members or acquaintances may have come through at different times. I had to gather this from different sources. It was quite a bit of work."

"Incredible. I'm so proud of you, Sharon." By now, his dinner roll had vanished, and he reached for another.

"I've included many stories, too. The hard part was knowing what to leave out. I've included an extensive bibliography. There's one whole chapter on the fire."

"What? Are you serious? I thought that the story about the fire was just part of the lore. Also, I'm thinking we should put a lock on Ebenezer's office door. His library is priceless."

Sharon just grinned. "You have to know where to look. Wouldn't you like to know what happened?" She teased, fiddling with her fork.

"Okay, spill." Alan leaned forward.

Sharon sipped her water. "There was suspicion that the fire was arson, but that was never proven."

"I'm afraid to ask," said Alan. "Did anyone die in the fire?"

"Yes, but there were more than forty slaves saved. Actually, they were called 'guests,' sometimes, not slaves."

"So, what happened?"

"Well, the fire was discovered by the pastor and another white man. Both of them lived near the church, and they happened to see the flames. It was night, of course. They rushed into the burning building and saved as many as they could. You'll read the whole story in my book."

"Oh my goodness! When will I get to see this masterpiece?"

"I have copies of the first draft, already at the editors. I'm hiring three editors. This is just too important to have errors."

"Good idea."

"We hope to have it published in hard cover. How many copies do you want?" Sharon grinned.

"Who, me?"

"No, I mean for the church. A hundred, a thousand?" Sharon asked.

"Not that many ... I have no idea," he admitted.

"Well, what I'm thinking is to do a pre-order."

"Like some celebrity?"

"Well, no," Sharon blushed a bit and looked away. "It's just that ... "

"Honey, that's a great idea. Then, we'll have some idea how many are needed. We need enough, but we don't want boxes of books sitting around gathering dust either."

A discreet tap on the door announced the waiter, who entered and delivered their meals. Alan suddenly realized he was starving. After a brief blessing, he fell to eating like a hungry refugee.

(Note: The complete novel, "Pastor G and the Haunted Church," by Dorothy May Mercer is available on Amazon. https://www.amazon.com/kindle-vella/story/B0BRGKM8B6)

Observations

I Watch the News

Dorothy May Mercer

The news: so appalling,
It's actually galling.
Events snowballing
Are terribly distressing
And downright depressing

(Gogyohka Poem 5 lines One phrase per line.)

Weeds

Linda Hawley

What's your favorite weed?
Mine is milkweed.
Because of the Monarch butterfly
I hold them high.
Otherwise, I don't like weeds.
They do not do good deeds.
What can I weed out of my life?
Good to eliminate strife.
Be nice to stop being lazy.
And sometimes a little crazy
Get rid of unhealthy habits.
That would be quite elaborate.

November

Gail Sheneman

November brought an 80-year birthday
for my former stepmother Lucy.
She is five years younger than I am,
But that doesn't matter at all, you see,

She and Daddy were married a year
and a half after Mama died.
He took her traveling all over,
Always keeping her by his side

He started taking her for granted
As along with him she'd ride.
She decided she'd had enough;
It was a matter of pride.

She and my dad parted ways and then
She married another man named Joe.
He stole her away from my dad
Who didn't want to let her go.

After Joe died she met Mr. Evans,
Who built her a beauty shop.
She thought that she was in Heaven,
And felt like she was on top.

When Mr. Evans died, she was lost but carried on
It was a blow cuz he was nice, she hated that he was gone.
Then at a dance she met O.J. Blount who was number five,
Had a three-story house, blueberries and honeybee hives,

The house he had built for him and his wife.
He thought they'd live there forever.
Until his poor wife died; she was gone like a feather.
The house was unfinished but built to withstand the weather.

Old Age

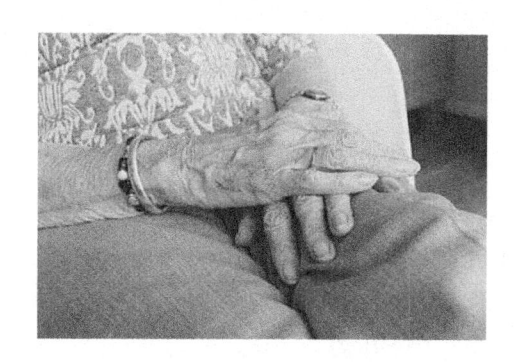

Raeanna Davidson

How old is old if you asked yourself this?
You would say old is the new young.
But some people would say that young is the new old.
But really, how can we know how old is old?

Truly, there is no way to tell how old is old.
If you look it up, it will tell you that the new old is the new young.
But we all are younger than we look.
Some people think we are old.

But the younger generation thinks everybody is young.
So, look in the mirror.
Ask, "Are you the young generation or the old generation?"
This was supposed to be funny.

But I lost what I was going to say at the end.
Old or the new generation?
Whatever you are, just know
You all are the younger generation in my book.

Words

Charleen Stroup

My words get lost sometimes
In the dark vault of my mind.
I'm searching for a lighted path
To guide and help me find

That certain, specific, unique and
Perfect description that states
Precisely what my stalling tongue
And mind are trying to locate

The eulogy for the lost expression
Is short and from the heart
With saddened loss and some despair
I'm tempted to just restart.

The energy of each word is like
A perfect talisman
That serves to guide and escort me
Away from Neverland.

By poking at the logjam that kept
My words stuck in my head
My thoughts begin to flow again
And with them go my dread.

At last, a poem begins to form
And like a springtime bouquet
I find the word to make the rhyme
And now I hope they'll stay.

Heavenly Love

Raeanna Davidson

Love is like air from above the heavens.
Also, love is from God the Father.
He gave us life to grow in our faith as we are God's children.

To love God the Father as He does for us
You are the light that shines on us.
The love God shows us, we show to others.

Faith on Sunday and every day;
We worship God the Father.
A little bit of everything God gives you.

Give God thanks and worship Him.
God is greater than you know.
God has love, faith, hope, joy, and peace on earth.

Holidays

Easter Bunnies

Gail Sheneman

A pile of Easter bunnies on a table
Are they real or is it just a fable?
Too many bunnies to put in baskets,
Many more than a tisket-a-tasket.

They're all for sale for one to five dollars
When you find one you want, give us a holler.
All are so beautiful from little to big,
Even the little one that looks like a pig.

They're fuzzy and pretty with long floppy ears,
So fluffy and puffy they bring me to tears.
Chocolate eggs all wrapped up in foil,
Hidden all over the yard (but not in the soil).

Little kids love bunnies and eggs but they do not know
It means that the Resurrection makes it all so.

Daylight Saving Time

Gail Shenemen

I had forgotten the time change was today.
I couldn't wake up as in bed I lay.
When I did wake up the clock showed ten to one
But it was nearly twelve—Daylight Saving
Time has begun.

Spring Forward, Fall Back I never can keep track. Why does it always come in November?

I can NOT ever remember, Makes no difference what the day, Daylight Saving is here to stay.

Maybe not, though! The time may come soon.
When one o'clock may always be noon.
Or noon may always fall back to one.
Either way I'll be so glad when it's gone!

A Letter to My Pen pal in Nigeria, Africa

Dorothy May Mercer

To: Netty Ejike
Mon, Jun 19 at 11:29 AM
Hi, Netty,

You asked what we did for Father's Day. Nice of you to ask. Several days in advance, I asked Dave what he would like for his Father's Day dinner. This would be on Saturday because Shelley and Tom were coming for lunch/dinner on that day. Dave's response was, "Steak, baked potatoes with sour cream and butter, tossed salad, and dessert."

Last fall we bought a 1/8 of beef from Wernette's Farms, a local farmer, had it butchered, processed, packaged, and stored in our freezer. (Wernette's grows beef cattle as a business. Her beef is safer, no hormones or chemicals, and more nutritious.) We had been saving two inch-thick, porterhouse steaks in our cache of beef for a special occasion. These are the best, most tender, pieces. And so, I thawed them out, and marinated them in the frig overnight. We have a small outdoor propane gas grill on our front deck. Tom is an expert on grilling. And so, Dave and Tom sat on the porch and grilled the steaks, while Shelley and I fixed everything else, and set the table inside. The steak turned out perfect, juicy, and pink in the center. Tom actually asked me for my marinade recipe. I told him I bought a package at the Dollar Store.

Dave and I had made the dessert the night before. It was a graham-cracker crust pie, filled with layers of cherry pie filling, vanilla pudding, and whipped cream. Totally decadent. I couldn't eat much of it--too sweet. But the men loved it.

How do you feel about that? Hmm? Hungry?

Let me tell you the story about what happened with the pie crust.

I'm not good at making graham cracker crust, so I bought one at the grocery store. It was perfect, nice and big, and unblemished. Getting it home is tricky, especially when you have a lot of groceries. But I was so careful, making sure it was set in a safe place in the back seat. And when I got home, I did not combine it with all the other stuff but gave it a safe spot all by itself.

Dave helped me to carry things. I warned him to be extra careful not to break the pie crust. So far, so good.

Come Friday night we unwrapped it carefully and set it on the counter all by itself, ready to go. Dave picked it up to brush a little crumb away, tipped it too much and made a mistake. Oh-oh. The whole thing slid right out into the sink and broke into pieces, like Humpty Dumpty.

My husband, who is always calm, cool, and collected, actually said a bad word.

I merely laughed. (That was a switcher-roo.)

It was too late. The store was closed. What to do?

I put as many pieces as I could rescue into the blender, added a half dozen graham crackers that I had in the cupboard and gave the whole thing a whirl. We added brown sugar and melted butter to the right consistency, packed the whole thing into a glass pie dish, and baked it in the oven.

Next morning I added the ingredients in layers and popped it into the frig for three hours.

I served it for dessert, and it was delicious.

Love,
Dorothy

Halloween Night

Linda Hawley

Too old for trick or treat
Let's walk down the street
To the black haunted house
We won't look for a mouse

We'll find a way to get in
I suppose this is a sin
We are looking for adventure
A goon may have us surrender

We'll find a secret passageway
And may not get out today
Captured by a spook
Hope we don't puke

Dead bodies we may find
We will leave those behind
And find a way to escape
Then we'll be in good shape

Funny Thanksgiving Story in 260 Words

Dorothy May Mercer

On Wednesday, November 22nd, the morning broke bright and sunny. Toward the lakeshore, the flock met to talk things over. Chief Waddleneck called the meeting to order. "We are gathered here to nominate our hero of the day," he began. "Do I hear a volunteer?"

Six wings went up. "Gobble, gobble," said the chief. "Please number off, one through six."

"One, two, three, four, five, six," shouted the young jakes.

"Miss Henny-penny will think of a number," said the chief.

She thought and thought. How to choose? Then she looked down and counted, "Aha, I have three claws. The winner is number three," she announced.

"Number three, please step forward," said Chief Waddleneck. Jake number three stuck out his chest and squeaked his version of a gobble. Proudly, he strutted toward the barn as the rest of the flock flew up into a tree.

Just then, Farmer Brown approached a chopping block while swinging a large sharp axe. He eyed Jake number three, "You're a bit scrawny," he observed. "Come here, you!"

"Yikes!" screamed Jake and began to run. "Help!"

"Oh, no, you don't," said Farmer Brown as he reached out with a long, wire hook. "Come here, you rascal." He swiped once toward Jake, grabbing hold of a wing.

Jake screamed in terror and flapped wildly. Suddenly, feathers flew, and Jake was free. Still flapping, tree andn the air, sailed into the tree, and landed next to the young Miss Henny-penny. She gave him a peck on the cheek while all the turkeys cheered.

"Our hero," they shouted and clapped their wings.

Suddenly, Jake found his grownup voice. "Gobble, gobble," he said and stuck out his chest.

Thanksgiving Blessing

Raeanna Davidson

Give thanks for everything God gave us
 Have a wonderful time with all your families.
God bless us with this food
That we are going to eat on Thanksgiving Day.
We bow our heads and give thanks for blessings of food,
and families
 and those who are not with us today.
We are thinking about you all on this Thanksgiving Day and every day.

Veterans's Day Memories

Dorothy May Mercer

The human mind is fascinating. Some memories stick for years. Others flash by and are instantly forgotten.

What simple act could have made a memory stick for seventy years? Perhaps it was the strength of the emotion. The first thing I remember of my time as a military spouse is the day the letter came. A simple white window envelope addressed to my husband. "Greetings," it said.

The Korean War was on. I was a new bride, madly in love with my young husband. We rented a home in Jackson, Michigan, for a tidy sum of $75 a month.

In those days, men wore the pants, working outside the home and supporting their wives. Women wore skirts and kept the house.

On that day, Dave was away, working at his job delivering milk door to door for Servall Dairy. Undoubtedly, I had spent the morning happily doing the routine household chores, but none of that sticks in my memory. The simple act of going to the door and fetching the mail comes to mind seventy years later. Why? I drew the letter from the little metal mailbox attached to our front door.

I remember how it felt when I held it in my hand—no words can describe that sinking feeling—despair, horror, terror, fear? No. I have felt that exact way only once in my life. It was more like a sledgehammer had hit my heart. It was the summons to military duty from the US government, called a draft notice, addressed to my nineteen-year-old husband. No need to open the letter. I already knew. "Greetings," it said …

Serving Our Country

Raeanna Davidson

God sees us on earth and in heaven.
He loves us so much that he gave us his son.
That one day, we will be up in heaven with our family.
When the time is right, no one wants to die,
But sometimes we do not have a choice.

It just happens to us.

Look at all the people who serve our country and all their families.
Some people do not get to see their families.
But I know that I am proud of them for serving our country.
God bless all of you who serve our country.

Jake's Christmas Editorial

Gerald Kinsey

Dear Readers,

Since I don't have anything useful to write about this week, let me share a story about an individual who had a Christmas wish that was granted.

Once upon a time there was a frog who wanted to see the world. Ever since he was a tadpole he looked forward to the day when he could explore the whole world. When his legs developed, he hopped out of the pond and went to the top of the nearest hill to see what he could see. No matter how high he jumped he could only see a short distance.

He soon began to feel dehydrated and returned to the pond to cool his heels. As he sat there in the comfort of the pond water, he tried to think how he could soar above the trees and see the rest of the world. He caught a few bugs with his tongue, and they tasted good, but how could he rise above his mundane existence?

Then a flock of birds flew overhead. It occurred to him that if birds could fly, why couldn't he? He hopped out of the pond and jumped as high as he could while flopping his legs. Of course, that didn't work. He just fell to the ground. Why couldn't he be a bird instead of a frog?

At that point an airplane flew overhead. Immediately the frog realized the solution to his problem. If people could fly using an airplane, so could he.

How could he get an airplane? Like most frogs he did not have an education in aerodynamics. He also didn't have any money to buy a plane. He thought about seeking employment to earn some money, but he gave up on that idea. If he went to the employment agency, he probably would not be able to get a job due to species prejudice. People just don't want to hire a frog.

Finally, he realized that the only way he could get an airplane would be to ask for one as a Christmas gift. Without any money to buy a postage stamp and with the cost of a stamp now being 66 cents he realized he could not depend on the United States Postal Service to deliver a letter to Santa Claus. Fortunately, he found an Arctic Tern who was flying to the North Pole, and he sent his request with him.

When Santa received the message, he referred it to a couple of twin elves who were in the aviation department of the Workshop. Their mother had really adored Santa and therefore, she named one of her sons Nicholas. The other was named after the town where they were born, which was Nacogdoches, Texas.

The elves tried to figure out how they could make an airplane that a frog could fly. No one had ever designed a plane for a frog before. After much debate, they decided they would need assistance from someone with more expertise. There was just one elf who they could ask. He was an Irish elf named Patrick. He normally went by the nickname Paddy. They didn't really want to deal with him because he was such a wacko, but they had no choice. They asked what they could do to provide an airplane for the frog. Paddy had several suggestions, but they didn't like any of them.

Finally, they concluded that they would have to take the matter back to Santa himself. He was in a bad mood because of all the labor strife at the Workshop. Half the elves were insisting that the whole operation needed to be taken to the South Pole due to global warming. The other half said that if the North Pole was good enough for Peter and Paul it was good enough for them.

Normally, Santa would be patient with any elves who had a question, but this was a really bad time to ask him to resolve a conflict. When asked what to do about the frog who wanted an airplane, he blurted out, "Nick, Nac, Paddy Wack, give the frog a drone."

They immediately saw that that was the solution. So it was that the frog achieved his desire to see the world, and he lived happily ever after until he was swallowed by a giant Burmese python a few days later. You would think with the drone he could have seen that coming. The moral of the story is this: Watch over your own home first before you try to oversee the rest of the world.

Jake

Gerald "Jake" Kinsey has recently published his third book, which is a true crime story about a famous murder case. He has been a dairy farmer, mobile home park operator, newspaper carrier and editor of the Lakeview Area news. He has also published, *The Poor Rich Man,* a story based on the Biblical account of the rich young ruler. *Him and Her*, Kinsey's book about survival in the Arctic, was illustrated by his granddaughter, Olivia Kinsey. He is interested in justice for the innocent.

Snowed Under ❄

Raeanna Davidson

As the nights grow longer and the air turns colder, winter is just around the corner for those of us in the Northern hemisphere. Some people hunker down and prepare to weather the storm, while others welcome the snow and icy wind with great excitement. Even if you can't wait for the coming spring, you must admit – there's something magical about winter.

 The buzz of the holidays, or even just that feeling of sitting in front of a fire for warmth while the wind howls outside, can't be beaten.

Let's all enjoy the weather and have a wonderful weekend. Stay safe and warm on this snowy day and drink coffee ☕, tea 🍵, hot chocolate ▢, hot water ♨, and hot apple cider 🍶.

2024 Resolution

Gail Shenemen

My resolution for 2024
Is something I've never done before.
I want to sort out some of my stuff.
You have to draw the line at enough.

I want to get a motorized trike.
But where would I ride it?
We only have a small sidewalk
And a patio beside it.

If I ride it on the highway
I will probably get run over
If I take it to the trail
I might have to use the motor.

Is it what I really, really want,
Or what I really, really need?
I've got a lot of choices to make.
In order for me to succeed.

First to know is can I afford it?
The answer to that I know is NO.
Maybe next year when more bills are paid
I'll have more money to show Joe.

He's afraid I'm running out of money.
And won't be able to keep my bills paid.
He's right, I am over-extended.
One of the biggest mistakes I've made.

I can't buy more 'til some of these are gone.
There's no more money coming in.
I've got to make what I've got last.
That's got to be my new resolution

People

The Auctioneer

Dorothy May Mercer

Today, when we think of the term "auction" it brings to mind a picture of elegantly dressed millionaires bidding on rare art objects at Sotheby's or Christie's auction houses, or of online auctions for collector's items. However, during my childhood, auctions were quite different. They were a social occasion for the family and the whole neighborhood. Growing up on a farm in the 1930s, during the time of the "Great Depression," meant there were very few opportunities for recreation. Life was nothing like it is today with its limitless choices.

There was no such thing as taking a vacation or retiring. People simply worked until they died. Poverty was no social stigma, as everyone was poor. The only movies people could afford were the summer Saturday night free movies on a grassy site downtown. We brought our own quilt made by my mother or grandmother and popcorn, grown on our farm. Recreation for us as children consisted of going to church on Sunday, occasional "visits" with relatives, the annual County Fair, and farm auctions.

When a farmer died, or went bankrupt, it was customary for the survivors to sell everything off by means of an auction. It being the early 1930s, bankruptcies were all too common. Sometimes the auction was conducted by the bank that held onto the poor fellow's mortgage.

The auction would be announced by a series of auction bills printed on cheap paper and posted around the county. They might be stuck onto retail store windows, tacked onto trees and fenceposts, or placed into mailboxes. Ads might be placed in local newspapers and advertising circulars. In addition to the location, date and time, headlines would list the most attractive items being sold. A long paragraph would include a more detailed list.

The star of the show would be the auctioneer, the rappers of the thirties. The best ones were like rock stars and could draw a crowd and a handsome salary, as well as a percentage of the profits. Their claim-to-fame was a rapid-fire, tongue-twisting lingo–the forerunner to todays' rap routines.

On the morning of the auction, Mother would be up early packing the wagon with the necessary equipment. It consisted of quilts for the kids, wooden folding chairs for the adults, and a picnic basket.

The day before, Dad would have culled a chicken from the flock and chopped off its head. After it finished flopping around, Dad hung it outdoors from the clothesline to bleed out. Next, he heated a large teakettle of water to the boiling point. While holding the dead chicken by its feet with one hand he poured the boiling water over the chicken feathers with the other hand. After a sufficient soak, the feathers would loosen enough so that Dad could strip the feathers off with his hand. I don't remember what he did with the feathers, but they were probably burned. Have you ever smelled burning chicken feathers? It is a distinctive odor. Dad would disembowel the bird and toss the guts into a "slop pail" to feed the pigs. Now the chicken was ready for Mother's magic.

149

The chicken' carcass must be thoroughly washed clean inside and out. Then, it was laid out on a cutting board and properly butchered, that is cut into exact serving pieces. The neck, back, gizzard, liver, and heart were set aside and saved for later use. Remember, this bird was culled from the flock? Ah, yes, it was not a tender young pullet. It was a tough old hen that have served out its life as a "layer." Any good farmer's wife knew how to turn this rejected piece of meat into a feast fit for a king.

Again, using only products from the farm such as water, corn meal, wheat flour and lard, along with seasoning and a few precious spices, Mother turned that meat into a delicious, fried chicken, picnic dinner. A hearty salad was made from farm products, as well. It included cold, cooked, potatoes and eggs, chopped radishes, onions, and cucumbers from the garden and pickles made in a big crock.

In addition to the food, Mother packed plenty of drinks in mason jars. Depending on whether there was money to buy lemons and sugar, she may have made freshly squeezed lemonade. Otherwise, she would have made sugary drinks flavored with five-cent packets of "Kool-Aid," which came in a variety of flavors, such as strawberry, raspberry, lemon, orange. lime, and grape.

Mother would send one of the boys to the icehouse to get a piece of ice that had been harvested from the lake during the previous winter. He would pull aside the burlap, scrape aside the insulating sawdust, and chop off a piece of ice with an ice pick. After rinsing the ice with water from the pump, he delivered it to Mother, clean and ready to be wrapped in a clean towel and placed in the bottom of the picnic basket. The serving dishes and mason jars would be nestled around the ice. Cups, plates, forks, linen napkins, and a tablecloth went next, topped off with a think towel tucked all around.

In those days, we did not have plastic wrap and disposables. Our only choice was wax paper and bread wrappers. "Boughten" bread came in waxed paper sacks, but most of our bread was baked at home. One of our staples was a large slice of homemade bread slathered with churned butter from our herd of milk cows. Mother may have included such bread slices, individually wrapped in wax paper. However, that was not a treat. What was a treat? Homemade cake, cookies, and fruit pie, or cinnamon rolls—any of which could be tucked into the picnic basket, depending on what was available in the kitchen cupboard.

We all piled onto the wagon, which was pulled by our team of horses. Usually, we did not take the more-comfortable buggy. Dad needed the wagon to transport any of his winning purchases and/or tow a large implement or a farm animal.

Upon arriving at the farm—the place of auction—our house would be unhitched and set out to graze and the wagon would be parked in a close-by field along with dozens of others.

Eagerly our family would unload the chairs, quilt, and picnic

151

basket, and proceed to the gathering place near the farmhouse and outbuildings. Dad would hurry away to greet his fellow farmers and wander through and around the wares displayed for sale. His job was to eyeball everything and surreptitiously make mental notes of the items on which he intended to bid.

Mother's job would be to stake out our spot with our chairs, quilt, and picnic basket, while enjoying a good old gabfest with the ladies. We kids were allowed to run free and play with our friends, so long as we didn't "get into trouble."

The sale might go on for hours, depending on the amount of stuff for sale. It likely included the entire household goods and furniture, as well as a plethora of farm implements and tools. Sometimes the farm itself would be auctioned off. Most of the livestock had been sold. Any thoroughbred breeding stock and horses were probably sold individually, while flocks and herds were sent to market. A few animals and birds might be left for the auction.

Timeout was announced for dinner hour. (Farmers ate dinner at noon, not lunch.) The auctioneer or proprietor would offer a blessing, while heads were bowed. This mealtime was a highlight of the day for the farm wives—a chance to display and compare their families, food, and quilts. There was much camaraderie, trading, and socializing.

The auctioneer's job was to entertain, entice, and set the pace and timing. He knew from experience which items would be bestsellers and how to build suspense and place those items to the best advantage. He would bundle items together for a variety of purposes. It might be to get rid of losers or simply to take care of bunches of small items in order to move things along. He knew how to eyeball and evaluate the onlookers, and keep his audience entertained with wisecracks, jokes, and patter. He depended on his loud voice and hand gestures. Megaphones were seldom needed.

Likewise, the crafty farmers knew what the auctioneer was up to and took pride in their ability to outsmart the opposition and snag a bargain.

The lucky winner paid for his goods immediately after the sale, with cash or check, and took the possession right away. Side deals were not unheard of, but there simply were no shenanigans. Everyone knew everybody and a man's sterling reputation was his pride. His solemn word was golden.

In those days, men's and women's roles and duties were clear. Whereas Mother spent most of her time enjoying relaxing and socializing, it was not unusual for her to have interest in some household goods that she needed or wanted. She had a small cache of money of her own and would use it very carefully. Whether to bid on a bundle of kitchen tools, a rocking chair, or a rare family heirloom, she knew how to get what she wanted and never fell for a "shiny object" the way Dad did.

Auctions were subject to the weather. A sudden summer rainstorm would send everyone scurrying to pick up their stuff and huddling under the tent. But the entertainment went on. A good auctioneer would be prepared with a selection of small items to auction off under the tent while the rain proceeded.

It didn't matter whether the auction was over or not, when Dad was ready to go, we would go. We gathered up their stuff, including any winning purchases, hitched the horses to the wagon, climbed aboard and headed home, happy, tired, and probably a bit dirty, too.

Earliest Memories of My Only Living Grandma

Dorothy May Mercer

Mama and I visited her kitchen. I think we got there from our farm home, riding in a horse and buggy. Together they were doing the "washing."

Later, after I got older, I learned that washing involved a number of steps. Water was brought up out of the ground with a hand pump and dumped into a huge, oblong, copper tub sitting on top of a wood stove. That water went into a washer along with lye soap.

I don't know what made the washer agitate, as there was no electricity.

Clothes went through a hand-operated wringer into the first round galvanized tub of rinse water and was squeezed and swished around by hand. Then the clothes went through the wringer into the second tub of rinse water, to which bluing was added. Finally, the clothes passed through the wringer into a clothes basket. The wringer mechanism was on a swivel, allowing it to be moved over each tub in succession. It was operated by a hand crank.

One woman fed the clothes through the wringer rollers, while the other woman turned the crank handle. Feeding the clothes properly was important so as to avoid popping a button.

The women carried the basket out the back door and hung the wet clothes on a clothesline, fastening them securely with clothespins. The white clothes were washed first. Next came the light-colored clothes, then the dark clothes and finally the dirtiest work clothes that the men wore. After each batch, the water became dirtier and darker in color as the dyes in the clothes would leach into the water.

The only thing I remember about my Grandmother Dodes was being on her kitchen floor, looking up at a dark skirt swirling

around two legs. I got in the way a lot. There were two women's voices, but words were just noise to me.
I did not understand many words.
Another day, sometime later, I remember clinging to my mother's skirt. Concerned, I looked up at her and wondered why Mama was crying. I had never seen Mama cry. I could tell we were outside in a scary place and there were a lot of people around. Some man's voice was coming from far away. I pulled on her skirt. "Sh," Mama said.
 I stood very still and worried because I didn't know what was happening. It was a funeral.
My grandmother, Millie Dodes, died in an automobile accident in 1934.

155

Oh, My Ron!

Linda Hawley

Oh, my Ron!
Handsome Don Juan
Flying his great love
Way up there above

Drove a big rig
Quite the thing-a-ma-jig
Manicures my lawn
Doesn't take him long

Florida in the winter
He'll message via Twitter
Adventures are bygone
Oh, my Ron!

Bob Hawley

Linda Hawley

Bob Hawley, Bob Hawley
On his bike pumping strongly
Bob Hawley, Bob Hawley
Posting pictures to tell a story

Bob Hawley, Bob Hawley
For a bargain he'd go to Milwaukee
Bob Hawley, Bob Hawley
If I find a bat, he says "call me"

Bob Hawley, Bob Hawley
Late night star gazing with coffee
Bob Hawley, Bob Hawley
Living to ninety

Mr. Negativity

Gail Shenemen

> He's always complaining.
> When it's not raining.
> But when it is raining,
> Again, he's complaining.

He'll say it's too hot,
Even when it's not.
Then he'll say it's too wet,
Can't mow the lawn yet.

> White skies hurt my eyes,
> He'll say too much blue in the sky.
> I love it when it's blue,
> But then it gets too hot, too!

When the sun doesn't shine
He thinks he'll get behind.
No sun again today,
He'll always say.

> But when it doesn't rain,
> Again, he'll complain.
> If I must hear it again,

I think I'll go (all the way) insane!

Butch and Marlene

Linda Hawley

Butch and Marlene
Everywhere they are seen.
Respected by their peers.
No one gives them jeers.
Did square dancing in their day
Had lots of fun at play
Live in a beautiful house
Both make an excellent spouse.
Could not have found finer
Not major nor minor.
The very best couple
They chuckle, bubble and cuddle

Shelley and Pastor Ron

Linda Hawley

So long Shelley and Pastor Ron
Happy trails to you the next road you're on
Enjoy the time whenever we meet
And love going out to eat
You paint a picture
With some words from scripture
Keep your religious view
May God bless you

Kathy

Gail Shenemen

There was a young lady named Kathy
Who was always very happy
The twelfth of May
Was her birthday
She was classy but never flashy.

She and her husband went on a trip
Down to Indiana to see their kids
At I-94 they got in a wreck
Wonder that it didn't break her neck
Just broke her ankle instead

She hobbled around on crutches for a while.
It was an effort just for her to smile
But always the lady
Our Kathy's no 'fraidy
She handled her "leader" job with style.

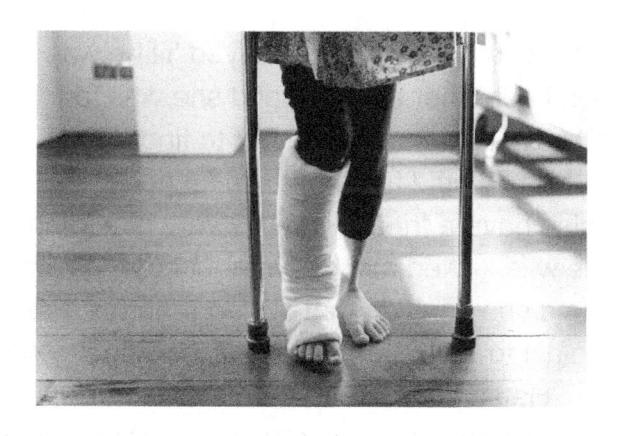

Molly

Gail Shenemen

I know a young lady named Molly.
She worked very hard for her money, by golly!
She was a bookkeeper for a store in town.
And she never ever let her boss down.
Molly is now a middle-aged lady.
She wanted very badly to have a baby.
She was married to a man who betrayed her.
To be alone she was so much "afraider"
His "lover" was a rider on his way to work.
A baby, he too, wanted, said the cruel dumb jerk.
He wanted Molly to have one and if she did,
He'd stay with her; if not, he'd split.

She was tall, slim, beautiful, and smart,
Any other man would have valued her heart.
She told me her tale; what could she do?
I said I would tell her, but she'd have to be true.
I asked if she'd ever heard of ovulation?
She said no so I gave her the explanation.
To our surprise, it really did the punch:
She was pregnant within the month!

She had a baby boy and he stayed 'til he was born,
Then he left her anyway, and she was forlorn.
She wanted me to help her to find a beau.
I said I would try to, and I'd let her know.
I also have a friend who is a very nice man.
His wife kicked him out without even a van.
I said she can't do that, it's your house, too.
I sold it to both, not just her and not just you!
He said it's okay, but I'm so alone.
Don't you know someone who can share my home?

I might but you'll have to come to my house to meet,
Then I'll introduce you and we'll go out to eat.
They arrived separately at my door.
But when I went to introduce them, my jaw fell through the floor!
He put his arms around her, bent her back.
And then he kissed her, a great big smack.
I said wait a minute! What's going on?
They looked at each other, then said shall we tell?
I said you've met before, right?
They said not before Friday night!

The mistake I made was to give them each other's number
They got right to it and did not slumber!
First, he called her, then she called him,
Then they called each other again,
On Saturday he visited her at home,
And on Sunday, they had dinner with her Mom.
So by Tuesday, when they were supposed to meet,
They had already had their greet and eat!

Elegy for Bethy

Gail Shenemen

There was a young lady named Bethy
Who only had two kids
Her son was in the Air Force;
He was good at what he did.

When she told me what had happened,
I thought somebody had died.
It was only that he had re-enlisted
That was a matter of pride.

He's only going to New Mexico
To start another hitch.
He's going to start another career,
And find a fitting niche.

He has a real sweet wife,
and a little girl and boy.
When he got discharged and came home
He brought Gramma Bethy so much joy.

Then suddenly, he re-enlisted,
Breaking Gramma Bethy's heart.
She wanted them to be close by
So she could play a part.

We tried to tell her it's not forever,
It's really for their own good;
New Mexico is just a flight away,
Then she finally understood.

Three hours on a plane
Without any rain
She could be there in less than a day.

I

Imagine

The Two Murders

E.L. Ward

After a week of searching, it proved hopeless. Having lost the rest of their flock in a blizzard, Edgar and Darcy Crow were finally left with no recourse but to abandon any thought of ever finding the others. They would have to join a *new* flock instead. It was heartbreaking, but a clear matter of necessity. The Scavenger's Almanac foreboded a lean winter. And Darcy was with egg.

Soaring on the frigid wind, it didn't take long after making the impossible choice to find their first prospects... a large gathering of crows down below, sifting through the husks of a stripped corn field. As they circled down, they were excited to note that several of the crows were congregated around the remains of some mid-sized animal, while the others browsed the barren ground. They took it to mean they were coming up on at least *two* flocks. *Two* prospective new families...

"We should try for the ones eating off the carcass," Edgar said to Darcy. "They look to be in pretty good shape. Strong and stout. I don't doubt they eat this well regularly."

"We can certainly *try*," she replied. "But you know how it is when a flock claims a meal. I doubt they're just waiting with open wings for a couple pot-lickers to come around."

"Heh, probably not," Edgar admitted. "But those other ones have even less to go around. They might run us off twice as fast."

"That's true." Darcy gave a long sigh. "Welcome to the joyous adventure of finding a new flock."

"Don't worry. We'll make it work somehow."

Doubtful as they were, hardly had they alighted on the ground when a crow from the flock on the carcass hopped up on a high stone, looking over all the others scattered in the field. Edgar, Darcy, and a number of others wandered towards him, intuiting that he had something to say...

"Alright everybody, listen up!" the crow on the rocky perch began. "You don't know it yet, but this could be a very big day for any one of you. No doubt, you've all heard of the Feint-Hop Murder. Well, that's us. And just in case you've been living under a rock, let me tell you a little bit about how we roll. We have one basic credo: We eat good, all year round... *every* year... every *night*... without fail. And only the choicest, fattest carnage will do. Going without or scraping by on produce ain't even in our vocabulary.

"So here's the deal. And mind you, this is the opportunity of a lifetime. We've talked it over, and we've decided that there's room in our flock for a few more. So if there's any strays out there... anyone unattached, or just looking to move up in the world... form a queue beside this rock. A few short questions and we'll know if you have the right stuff to join up. Don't miss this chance!"

"*Wow*," Edgar and Darcy heard, seeing another awed onlooker had silently come up next to them during the little speech. "Those guys are really something."

"Apparently..." Edgar agreed a bit doubtfully. "Sounds like exactly what we're looking for. Almost too good to be true."

"Really?" the stranger asked. "You're looking for a flock too? Are you guys lost, the same as me?"

"Well, you could say that," Darcy replied, a bit low and sympathetic. "We got separated. Is that what happened to you?"

The other crow took a while considering his answer, appearing to stare off rather blankly for a time. "Yeah... I think so," he answered thoughtfully. "I'm not sure what happened. One morning I woke up, and everybody was gone. I don't know where they went."

Edgar and Darcy exchanged a look, as well as a dark theory as to what had become of this poor fellow's flock. "What's your name, buddy?" Edgar asked at length.

"Simpson," the stranger answered.

"Well, Simpson," Edgar continued, "why don't you go on ahead of us in line? We've got each other, at least. But it sounds like you've got nobody. So I think you should get first crack at joining up with that flock."

Simpson nodded his beak energetically. "Oh, thank you, Sir! Ma'am! You guys are nice folks!"

They watched him hop away, eventually following with a sullen lethargy. They didn't feel they'd really done him any favors. It seemed a foregone conclusion that letting Simpson go first wasn't going to help his odds very much, getting into what sounded like a pretty upscale flock. Not that their own chances were much better...

After a bit of a wait, Edgar and Darcy were ushered around the stone. They caught sight of Simpson fluttering away, just as they heard the two interviewing crows snickering amongst themselves...

"Now dare's a brain trust," one quipped.

"The look on his face when we asked him that math question! Classic," the other agreed. "Today's our lucky day."

Edgar cleared his throat, and not just to get their attention. There was a dandy lump forming in it.

"Hello," Darcy added weakly, as they looked back with unimpressed eyes.

"Yo," one said. "Lookin' to join the Feint-Hop Murder, eh? What's special about the two a youse?"

"Special?" Edgar asked, almost laughing it off. "I don't know if you'd say there's anything *special* about us. My name is Edgar Crow, and this is my wife, Darcy Crow. We... we just lost our old flock, and..."

"...Ugh, another charity case," the second interviewer interjected. "Sorry buddy, but we're going to have to stop you right there. We have very particular qualifications for joining up with our Murder. It's a highly exclusive club. We rate every bit as good as advertised. Now, if you've got nothing to bring to the table but a sad story, then I'm sorry, but this isn't going to work out."

"I... I don't know what you want from us, honestly," Edgar stammered. "We're able-bodied and keen-sighted. We can pull our own weight just like anyone. Only we need the security of a flock. You see, Darcy's about to lay and egg, and..."

"...Doublin' down on the hard luck ain't gonna help, pal," the first interviewer insisted. "Fact is, we don't need ya. Betta luck next time."

Edgar looked between the two of them, loath to give up. But there was clearly nothing for it. A sad story really *was* all they had at this point...

"Alright," he said. "We won't take up any more of your time. I... I guess I hope you find whatever it is you're looking for."

"I suspect we already did. The one who came around just before you should be a nice fit for us."

This response puzzled Edgar. But he did as he said and left them to their business without another word. He and Darcy fluttered off out of earshot, not far afield from Simpson.

"Well, that didn't go so well," Edgar sighed.

"Maybe it's just as well." Darcy shrugged her wings. "They didn't seem very pleasant."

It was about this time that Simpson noticed them and flew excitedly into their midst. "Hi there!" he said.

"Hi, Simpson," Darcy said a bit morosely.

"Guess what? I got in! I... I thought I didn't do so good at their questions, but they said I could join anyway! Isn't it great?"

"Sure it is, Simpson; we're happy for you," Edgar replied earnestly enough. "Sounds like you'll be eating well this winter."

"Well, what about you guys?" Simpson asked. "Did you answer their questions too? Are we going to be flock-mates?"

"I'm afraid not," Darcy said. "They told us they didn't need us right now."

"Oh..." Simpson whimpered. "Well that's really too bad. You guys are so nice. They should've let you join."

"Don't worry about us; we'll be alright," Edgar assured him. "Maybe we'll see you around some time."

Simpson nodded with refreshed joy. "Yeah, that'll be great. Take care, Simpson," Darcy said. They each turned their own way - Simpson to his new flock, and Edgar and Darcy toward the barren field. The two of them had reached the point of being inconsolable... facing hunger and loneliness for themselves, and unable to fight a nagging concern for their new friend. Those few representatives they'd encountered of the so-called 'Feint- Hop Murder' had indeed been coarse. What they wanted with Simpson was a foreboding mystery...

"Don't despair, neighbors and countrymen," they heard suddenly. The voice of an old crow, bent and scanning the ground nearby, called out to them. "Your travails today need not be counted vain. That which you came here seeking may still be yours."

Edgar and Darcy hesitated, unsure how to respond to a fancy statement like that coming out of nowhere. "H... hello," Edgar said. "What's your name, Sir? And what do you mean? We came here hoping to find a new flock, but they turned us out. I don't think there's anything we can do... unless you mean to say something on our behalf. Are you with them?"

"No, not with *them*," the old crow laughed, even as he went on poking through the fallen corn stalks. "As for my name, it is Hilliard. The offer I make you is my own, as an elder in a flock of quite a different sort than theirs. And while I don't mean to be presumptuous, let alone braggadocious, I think you might find our invitation even more to your liking."

"Really? More to our liking than all the meat we can eat every day?" Edgar asked a bit playfully.

Hilliard chuckled again. "Well, I'm afraid we can't so much rival their extravagances. Sometimes, there is feasting. Other times are leaner. But we remember what we are... what we were designed to be. We are scavengers... made to withstand times of little, as well as plenty. We trust the Maker. And there is always enough." Just then, he turned up a buried cob with his beak. "So I say, you may go with us. You will be most welcome. For that is *our* specialization. Fellowship... hospitality. To us, a full heart is worth more than a full stomach."

Edgar and Darcy liked the sound of this very much. But at the same time, a different uncertainty plagued them. Hilliard was gracious, but very old and unknown to them. They looked out into the field, and while they could see a good number of crows still picking about, there was nothing conclusively tying Hilliard to any of them. They deplored thinking so pragmatically, but for all they knew, the "flock" he spoke of could be nothing more than memories that lived on in a tired old mind. Suffice it to say, they were skeptical...

But before they could formulate some polite request to be introduced to the others in the flock, they were surprised by a harsh call...

"Hey! Hey you!" crowed a plump younger fellow, whizzing in from the direction of the interview rock. "You said your name was Edgar Crow?"

"...Yes..." Edgar answered meekly. "What does...?"

"...As in, Edgar *Allen* Crow?" the fellow interrupted, being joined by two more crows of even more impressive bulk. "The famous sports legend?! The guy that pioneered lid sledding?!"

"Heh..." Edgar snickered nervously. "Well, okay, you got me. I was pretty adventurous in my younger days. But that seems like forever ago now..." His eyes glinted warmly back at Darcy. "Ever since I found somebody worth settling down for."

"Yeah, yeah... family life... whatever," the young crow said. "Anyway, I'm sure you're all washed up now; I get that. The main thing is: You *used* to be somebody!"

"*Okay*..." Edgar replied. "Well... what about it?"

"We were talking it over with Cheswick and Vernon over there," he began to explain, nodding back at the stone. "And when I heard the name you gave, I realized those morons were way too hasty throwing you out on your ear. A famous has-been could be huge for the Feint- Hop Murder! Celebrity endorsement!"

Edgar worked a moment to sift through all the derision and get at the basic gist of the whole conversation. "So... are you saying we're in after all?"

"That's exactly what I'm saying, Pops!"

"Really?" Darcy inquired further. "I mean, are you sure? Did you clear it with your elders?"

"Ha!" one of the other young crows squawked. "*Elders*? Look, lady: You don't know who you're talking to. This is Castro of the Feint-Hop Murder, his own self. He makes the decisions around here."

"Huh..." Edgar said doubtfully before he could stop himself. "That is, I've never met such a young flock leader before."

"Well, how else do you think we reached such heights as a Murder?" Castro asked. "You gotta get all those old people with their old ideas out of office as soon as possible if you want to make real progress."

"So, what do you say?" one of Castro's proverbial 'bodyguards' asked. "Do you want into the Murder, or don't you?"

"The *Murder*..." Edgar repeated a bit laboriously. "Quite attached to the name of your group, aren't you?" It wasn't the most agreeable thing to point out, but he felt genuinely preoccupied by their branding mentality.

"Sure we are!" Castro agreed enthusiastically. "Murder, Murder, Murder! We don't shy away from the technical term for a flock of crows. Not one bit. In fact, we embrace it. But you'll find out more about that soon enough. So, you in?"

Edgar and Darcy exchanged another look. Even with the promise of bountiful food for themselves and their chick on the way, nothing about this choice was easy. To tell the truth, they were completely gridlocked. It wasn't until Simpson suddenly flew up to them that they had any clarity. There was at least one other person in this 'Murder' they felt confident they could get along with. And anyway, they had a more and more distinct feeling that he might need them. So finally, and reluctantly, they agreed...

"Yes," Edgar said. "Yes, I think we are."

"Terrific!" Castro exclaimed. "In that case, I'd say we've reached our quota." He turned to his bodyguards. "Go round everyone up. Let's find dinner."

"Sure thing, Boss." They took off and returned to the clean-picked bones of the carcass.

"Did you say dinner?" Simpson asked. "That sounds good."

"It will be, little buddy," Castro said, taking Simpson under his wing. "And you're going to play a starring role in getting it."

"*I am*?" Simpson marveled. "Yes. I'll explain it all when we find a good spot." Edgar and Darcy overheard this, of course, feeling their already sunken guts sink even deeper. But just then, they heard Hilliard's voice behind them...

"There now," he said. "It was quite without need that you lost hope. Far from being forsaken, you were even given a *choice*. A rare thing indeed, in such need."

"I just hope you're not too disappointed with what we chose," Edgar replied.

"It's nothing personal," Darcy added. "And it wasn't an easy choice."

Hilliard nodded. "I understand. I do not doubt that you've done what seems best for your growing family. But I would have you know this, before you go, that you may bear it in mind: My flock and I plan to graze this field for the next two days. So if, in the course of that time, you should wish to seek me out for anything, you'll know where to find me."

It didn't immediately occur to Edgar or Darcy what that was supposed to mean... but after just a bit of thought, it seemed clear enough. "Well, thank you very much for that," Edgar finally said. "I guess if you don't see us in the next few days, you'll know we're getting along well enough."

"Indeed," Hilliard agreed. "Godspeed to you, neighbors and countrymen."

***

"Alright, this is it," Castro explained as he led Simpson on. "No pressure. Just get out there and do everything I told you, and when you're finished, we'll all have a warm meal."

"I don't know," Simpson replied. "This isn't like anything I've ever heard of before. I don't understand. How does it all lead up to us finding food?"

"Oh, you'll see," Castro answered. "Get this right, and I promise you'll see in a *hurry*." He looked down the road, making an excited little hop when he noticed a great big truck coming. "Okay, this is perfect timing! Hop out there now! Now! And don't forget to make a big show of that broken wing."

"But I don't have a broken wing," Simpson groaned.

"I know that, you nitwit! I told you to *pretend*! Now get out there, before I give you a real one!"

Reluctantly, Simpson bounded out into the road, while the rest of the flock watched expectantly... Edgar and Darcy most urgently of all. They hadn't heard much of Castro's gambit and didn't immediately understand what business he had sending Simpson out onto a road with a truck coming. Poor Simpson looked every bit as incredulous as they were, even as he managed to pull off a pretty good broken wing routine. He turned back to Castro...

"Okay... what do I do *now*?"

"*Ugh*..." Castro sighed. "The *dog*, remember? It's all about the dog in the yard. You have to get his attention. Then you have to fly when I tell you to fly. Not before."

"But how do I get his attention?"

"However you want!" Castro fumed. "Call him a mangy cat! Insult his mother! Just so long as you really rile him up!"

"Well, okay..." Simpson turned back and cupped his 'good wing' to his beak, winding himself up to call into the yard across the street from the Murder. "Hey... dumb dog! Over here! Look at me, you dumb dog!"

Sure enough, this proved adequate to wake the great big Boxer from slumbering in his doghouse. The feral beast made a very impressive display of his teeth as he slowly began to advance on Simpson...

"Keep it up; you're doing great!" Castro coached in a hoarse whisper. "Insults are a bit lackluster, but hey, it's working!"

Finally, Edgar could stand it no longer. At the very least, he would have to question his new leader about all this monkey business. He crept over to Castro...

"Say, what's the big idea here?" he asked quietly, not quite bold enough to spoil the act before he so much as understood it. "Putting Simpson out in the streets like this, picking fights with house pets? What gives? If this is some stunt you're used to pulling off, why not have someone with more experience out there?"

"Hey now, superstar," Castro riposted. "Why not have a little more faith in your friend? He can do it. And anyway, the rest of us have had our fill. What do you think we chose him for in the first place? We need somebody that'll do what he's told. Somebody who's too simple to say no."

Before Edgar could object, they were both diverted by the sound of a bark and a rolling growl.

"Yipe!" Simpson exclaimed as he hopped back, mere feet away from the mongrel. "Can... can I fly away now?!"

"Get out of there, Simpson!" Edgar called.

"*No*! Not yet!" Castro insisted. "Sidestep! Dodge him! Just stay out there a little longer!"

Suddenly, the escalating chaos exploded with the sudden blaring of a loud horn. Simpson and the dog froze stiff.

"Now!" Castro called. "Fly now!!"

Just in time, Simpson leapt and fluttered. The enormous eighteen- wheeler went careening through the very space he'd occupied half a moment earlier. The Feint-Hop Murder crowed and cackled their delight. Edgar and Darcy only looked on, horrified...

Moments that felt like hours passed, before Edgar and Darcy finally emerged from their trance enough to see the fruits of all of Simpson's reckless endangerment. Dog meat was on the menu, and dinner was served. Tasty as it would've looked in any other instance, it only served to turn their stomachs. This was the answer to all the riddles. Their new *Murder* was precisely that.

"Mm, great dinner... uh... what was your name?" Castro mumbled through his full beak. "Simpleton?"

"Simpson," Simpson replied.

"Right, well, good job," Castro congratulated him. "I gotta say though, you cut it pretty close at the end there."

Another crow laughed. "Not as close as the last guy."

"Heh, yeah," Castro chuckled. "Funny thing... I can't seem to remember his name, either."

"That, I couldn't tell ya. But I'll always remember him as 'Side-Dish'." They all laughed at that. "What's a matter with you twos?" another asked, looking at Edgar and Darcy. "Ain't ya hungry?"

Neither really knew how to respond. They were, at once, the most and the least hungry they'd ever been. "It's just..." Edgar tried. "Well... I mean... don't get us wrong: We love eating dead animals. We've just never been an accessory to their dying before."

177

"Kind of exceeds our mandate as scavengers a bit, don't you think?" Darcy added.

Castro shrugged his wings. "Maybe. But so what? When nature doesn't give, we just take. That's what sets us apart." He looked down at the feast. "Now where's the spleen in all this? I gotta have me some spleen."

"You got the spleen last time," one of them objected.

"I get the spleen *every* time," Castro clarified. "Comes with the territory of being in charge. Get with the program, Thorsten, or you'll wake up one of these days with your eyes pecked out."

Bickering and squabbling over various organs continued on and on until it was nothing more than a droning to Edgar and Darcy. For what seemed the umpteenth time that day, they exchanged a doubtful look. Perhaps the most doubtful they'd ever managed.

***

"We've thrown in our lot with a bunch of psychopaths," Darcy mentioned sometime after dusk, when the two of them were withdrawn enough to speak of such things.

"I know," Edgar sighed his agreement. "But what are we supposed to do about it now?"

"I say we ditch them," Darcy suggested. "We still have Hilliard's offer. He must've known it would come to this."

"I agree. But it's not that simple. We can't leave Simpson behind. They'll just keep using him until one day, he doesn't get out of the way fast enough."

Darcy shook her head dejectedly. "You're right. We have to spring him, too. But how? He's indispensable now. Castro's not going to let him out of his sight."

Edgar pondered this briefly, noticing that the rest of the flock was currently engaged in helping itself to a hardy second dinner. "Maybe we're getting all worked up about nothing again," he mused. "These people eat like no tomorrow." He turned back to Darcy. "And you know what comes after a day of feasting..."

Darcy nodded. "Food coma."

Sure enough, within an hour, the whole Murder was out cold, sawing big, noisy logs. Edgar and Darcy didn't even have to tread light on their talons. They hopped right up to Simpson and nudged him with their beaks...

"Wha...what?" Simpson asked drowsily.

"Simpson, it's me... Edgar," Edgar whispered. "Wake up. We're getting out of here."

"We... we are?" he gasped. "But why?"

"Because, these guys are terrible," Darcy explained. "They have no regard for anything. And they weren't very nice to you."

"They were kind of nice to me after I got the food," Simpson qualified. "They said I was a hero and stuff."

"I'm sure they did," Edgar quipped. "But be honest with yourself, Simpson. After what they had you do, do you really *feel* like a hero?"

Simpson hung his beak. "Well... no."

"Of course you don't," Darcy encouraged. "You're much too kind and thoughtful to fit in here. You should come with us. There's another flock we can join. They don't feast every day, but they won't put you up to hopping in front of dogs and trucks anymore, either."

Simpson yawned, fluffing out his feathers. "That sounds good. So, where do we go?"

"Right back to where we started," Edgar answered, grinning as much as his beak allowed. "Come on; follow us!"

***

Early the next day, Edgar stuck a slick landing—not at all unlike those he had perfected in his sledding days—depositing another chunk of corn cob on the ground near the rest. He was tired, and starving, but never more delighted to do the honest work of scavenging. As soon as his cob rolled to a stop, Hilliard nodded his approval.

"I'm not specially gifted at arithmetic, but I do believe that will be enough for everyone," he said.

Edgar looked up and around at his new flock. Far from just Hilliard and his imagination, there were almost twenty in their group... bright faces, all, though their feathers were jet black. "Music to my ears," Edgar said. "I don't know if I've ever been so hungry."

"But of course, it won't be tasty," Hilliard reminded them. "You know corn in the winter. Hard, dry, bland. I do hope you don't come to regret your defection to our side."

Darcy shook her head. "Don't worry about that. We'll take this over dog meat any day."

"Still..." Hilliard pondered. "I'm given to wondering if there might not be something we could learn from those young hooligans."

"*Pfft*," Edgar replied. "I'm sure you're joking. What could you possibly learn from them?"

"Well, take, for instance, the value of *branding*. It occurs to me we've never named our flock. Perhaps with an appealing moniker, we might dissuade others more effectively from joining the rather unsavory bands. The trouble is: what name to choose? 'The Kind Murder'? 'The Pleasant Murder'? 'The Hospitable Murder? Oh, I'm afraid I'm not much gifted at this."

"Maybe you'll come up with something better after breakfast," Darcy suggested.

"Well, whatever you pick," Simpson interjected, "I think I'd like it better if it didn't have the word 'Murder' in it."

Edgar nodded enthusiastically. "Yeah. I'll go along with that."

"Very well," Hilliard agreed. "Murder is out. The rest will be decided later. But for now, let us eat!"

The as-yet-unnamed flock of crows all gathered round their dry corn cobs. They gave thanks... they ate... they shared stories and laughter. Of course, they didn't have quite so much as to completely stuff themselves. But it was enough. And if it didn't really taste so great, no one managed to notice.

Better is a dinner of vegetables where love is, than a fatted calf and hatred therewith.

Luke

The author, E.L. "Luke" Ward, lives in Michigan with his two dogs. He has created a humorous fantasy world in his books. *The Chocolate Prophecy*, introduces Jek, who is on a quest trying to solve the mystery of the Chocolate Prophecy. His next books feature Horace Templar, a Perry Mason-ish/jackal public defender. The Horace Templar series includes *Horace Templar and the Case of the Draft-Dodging Drone* and *Horus Templar and the Case of the Dubious Decedent,* as well as other books. Our hero, Horus, has amazingly humanistic qualities as he embarks on fantastic exploits.

E.L. Ward's popular books are available on Amazon.com and on display in book stores, libraries, and book fairs in West Michigan.

Four Limericks

Dorothy May Mercer

There was a young lady from Dumas
Who went out to plant some petunias
She tripped on a crack, and injured her back
And dirtied her brand new Bermudas.

There was an old man from Kelarden
Who went out to tend to his garden
Fell into a hole and cracked his elbow
He quickly said, "I beg your pardon."

There was a sweet child from North Tracy
Who went out to harvest a daisy
She started to run and fell on her thumb
'Twas thought that her action was crazy

There once was a cat named My Diddler
Who stretched, yawned, and pawed in his litter
Uncovered a treat, which he swiftly did eat
And forgot he was planning to sit there.

Fly

Gail Sheneman

In my dreams I fly; I can soar so high.
I just flap my arms and
go, and oh, I love it so!
I wish that I could really
fly, way up in the sky.
I love to fly!
I could fly so far,
maybe I could reach
a star,
I hope that when I
die, I can really fly.
I love to fly!

Made in United States
Orlando, FL
30 May 2024